AF708347

WOMEN, PUBLIC LIFE AND DEMOCRACY

COMMONWEALTH PARLIAMENTARY ASSOCIATION

The CPA is an association of Commonwealth parliaments and legislatures whose Members, irrespective of gender, race, religion or culture, are united by community of interest, respect for the rule of law and human rights and freedoms, and the pursuit of the positive ideals of parliamentary democracy.

The Association mobilizes this diverse grouping of 16 000 Members of approximately 175 national, state, provincial and territorial Assemblies into a Commonwealth parliamentary community which shares its experiences and expertise to enhance the governance not just of its own people but of all nations. By fostering improved understanding of both the democratic process and of policies and legislation in other jurisdictions, the Association promotes the continuing advancement of constitutional structures, parliamentary practices and procedures, and policy formulation. It also contributes to the professional development of Parliamentarians and parliamentary staff.

The CPA brings Parliamentarians together through an extensive annual programme of conferences, seminars, workshops, study groups, inter-parliamentary exchanges, and publications and information services. Included in this programme is the publication of books such as this that enable parliamentary practitioners to contribute to the published body of knowledge in the field of representative governance and political theory.

Founded in 1911, the CPA is based in London and has a network of branches in fifty-two of the fifty-four nations of the Commonwealth.

Also available

The Overseers: Public Accounts Committees and Public Spending
David G. McGee, QC

Women, Public Life and Democracy

Changing Commonwealth Parliamentary Perspectives

Compiled and edited by
Joni Lovenduski and Rosie Campbell with
Jacqui Sampson-Jacent

Commonwealth Parliamentary Association
in Association with
Pluto Press
London · Sterling, Virginia

First published 2002 by Pluto Press
345 Archway Road, London N6 5AA
and 22883 Quicksilver Drive, Sterling, VA 20166-2012, USA

www.plutobooks.com

Copyright © 2002 Commonwealth Parliamentary Association

The rights of Joni Lovenduski, Rosie Campbell and the Commonwealth Parliamentary Association to be identified as the authors of this work have been asserted by them in accordance with the Copyright, Designs and Patents Act 1988

British Library Cataloguing in Publication Data

A catalogue record for this book is available from the British Library

Library of Congress Cataloging-in-Publication Data

Women, public life and democracy : changing Commonwealth parliamentary perspectives / compiled and edited by Joni Lovenduski, Rosie Campbell and the Commonwealth Parliamentary Association.

p. cm.

Preface – Women, public life and democracy – Introduction – Setting out the terms / by Prof. Joni Lovenduski – The Role of Parliamentarians – Representation without the incumbency barrier: the example of Scotland – Waving goodbye to dinosaurs: the Northern Ireland Women's Coalition – Making Parliamentarians listen to women voters and getting women elected – The Beijing process – Gender mainstreaming Affirmative Action: help or hindrance? – Education and sex equality equalising access to care and services – The Nordic model: The Example of Finland Equality Policy. The example of Malaysia : the implementation of equal rights legislation / by Hon. Gillian James – Does size matter? sex equality in small states – How can NGOs lobby for change? A Users guide / by Georgina Ashworth – Improving access to credit, technology and business – Can the media be resexed? / by Jackie Ashley – Conclusions / by Rosie Campbell – What works and what does not for women in politics? a Commonwealth perspective / by the Commonwealth Parliamentary Association – Institutional framework for mainstreaming gender in public service personnel management / by the Commonwealth Secretariat Affirmative Action in the Commonwealth Secretariat – Part 2. Gender-sensitizing Commonwealth Parliaments: report of a CPA Study Group, February-March 2001 / by Mrs Jacqui Sampson-Jacent – Gender-sensitizing Commonwealth Parliaments: Commonwealth Parliamentary Conference Plenary report, September 2001 – Report of a Commonwealth Parliamentary Conference Workshop on Gender, September 2001 – Strategic partnerships for politics in the 21st Century : Report of a Commonwealth Women Parliamentarians Meeting, September 2001 – Representation of Women in Commonwealth Parliaments and Legislatures.

ISBN 0-7453-2039-2

1. Women in politics–Commonwealth countries. 2. Women's rights–Commonwealth countries. I. Lovenduski, Joni. II. Campbell, Rosie, 1967- III. Commonwealth Parliamentary Association.

HQ1236.5.C7 W66 2003
306.2'082–dc21

ISBN 0 7453 2039 2 hardback

Designed and produced for Pluto Press by
Curran Publishing Services, Norwich

Printed and bound in the European Union by
Antony Rowe Ltd, Chippenham and Eastbourne, England

Contents

PART 2

Tables

Preface

Fifty-six female and male Parliamentarians from more than thirty Commonwealth and other countries met from 19–23 June 2000 at a conference on Women, Public Life and Democracy held by the Commonwealth Parliamentary Association (CPA), in co-operation with the British Council, at Wilton Park in the United Kingdom. The delegates reviewed developments in the position of women in society and identified successful strategies employed throughout the Commonwealth and elsewhere in order to bring about economic, social, political and cultural equality between the sexes.

With the broad framework of the theme of women and democracy, delegates explored and discussed progress on sex equality in the twelve main areas that were identified by the Fourth World Congress on Women at Beijing in 1995: poverty, education and training, health, violence, armed conflict, the economy, power and decision-making, institutional mechanisms for the advancement of women, human rights, the media, the environment and the girl child.

While no delegates were satisfied with progress in their country, almost all reported progress. Nevertheless, resistance to equality between the sexes continues to impede the access of women not only to political power, but also to cultural, social and economic resources. The low numbers of women in Parliament are a sensitive indicator of what happens elsewhere in democratic systems. The challenge for governments and women's advocates is to break down resistance to women's rights and to develop comprehensive programmes of sex equality that are backed by widespread public support: that is, support both from men and women.

The first part of this book, which stems from the CPA–British Council conference at Wilton Park, offers examples of such programmes and discusses their success and progress. Based on the discussion papers made available by the main speakers, it is built on the proceedings of the conference. It includes points made by participants in the discussions. In compiling this volume we have acted as editors rather than authors. Our aim has been to reproduce the conference deliberations, debates and conclusions in a form that is accessible to the community of Parliamentarians, non-governmental organizations, advocates, activists, experts and citizens who are interested in progress to sex equality.

The second part of this book takes progress in the parliamentary field a step further. It begins with the report of the CPA Study Group on 'Gender-sensitizing Commonwealth parliaments' written by the Clerk of the Trinidad and Tobago House of Representatives, Mrs Jacqui Sampson-Jacent. The Study Group was set up following a suggestion made by the Commonwealth Women Parliamentarians, a group within the CPA, that it is necessary to examine conventions and language embedded in parliamentary standing orders that possibly affect behaviour and attitudes towards women. The focus of the Study Group was broadened to include consideration of other aspects of parliamentary life that many women find alienating or difficult. The Group, composed of eight Commonwealth women Members, met in Kuala Lumpur, Malaysia, from 25 February to 2 March 2001.

The report then served as a background paper for discussions of the gender issue at the September 2001 Commonwealth Parliamentary Conference held in Canberra, Australia, which was attended by close to 520 Members and officials of 156 Commonwealth parliaments and legislatures. Summary reports of those discussions follow the Study Group report, as delegates considered the subject first in plenary session and then in detailed discussions in a workshop. A meeting of the Commonwealth Women Parliamentarians held during the conference also considered the subject as part of a broader agenda on action to advance the representation of women in Commonwealth parliamentary houses, and those deliberations are also summarized here.

The two parts of this book provide an insight into the way in which Commonwealth parliaments and legislatures are evolving new perspectives based on representation, gender and the involvement of women at all levels in parliamentary democratic institutions.

PART 1

1 Introduction: setting out the terms

Joni Lovenduski

In this chapter the arguments for the political equality of women and men are set out and the main terms used in defining sex equality are explained. This chapter introduces many of the arguments that are made later on in the book. It begins with a definition of political representation.

Political interest in women's representation is founded on ideas about citizenship, equality and representation and located in discourses about power, democracy and gender.

> Political representation is primarily a public, institutionalized arrangement involving many people and groups, and operating in the complex ways of large-scale social arrangements. What makes it representation is not any single action by any one participant, but the overall structure and functioning of the systems, the patterns emerging from the multiple activities of many people. It is representation if the people (or a constituency) are present in governmental action, even though they do not literally act for themselves.
>
> (Pitkin 1967: 222)

In this quotation Pitkin encapsulates the complexity of political representation and raises the question of the kind of presence that is necessary for representation to take place. Many feminists have claimed that only when women are present in decision-making in proportion to their membership of the population are they adequately represented. This claim has at its heart the notion that women should represent women. It raises the question of whether what is said is ever separable from who is speaking. It challenges systems of representation in which groups of the population are consistently excluded from representative assemblies and committees.

Pitkin distinguishes between various kinds of political representation. One of her distinctions is particularly useful, and was echoed in the discussions at Wilton Park. Her distinction between descriptive and substantive representation may be simply described as follows: descriptive representation refers to the quantity of representation, in the sense of the numbers of women who are present in decision-making positions or deliberative fora. Substantive representation is about what and whose issues and perspectives get represented. We might therefore think of it as qualitative representation.

The understanding of gender itself has been subject to important changes. In particular, it has become common to distinguish between the concepts of sex and gender in political discourse. Yet there is considerable confusion between the terms. Some clearly regard them to be interchangeable whilst others make complex distinctions between them. Although the most arcane elements of research definitions of gender are probably not useful in lay discussion, a good working distinction can help to clarify political discussion.

The concept of sex is usefully understood as a dichotomous variable separating the categories man and woman. The term gender may be thought of as social construction of biological sex. Accordingly we can define gender as a characteristic of both women and men that is expressed in relations that are embodied in the sexual division of labour, compulsory heterosexuality, discourses and ideologies of citizenship, motherhood, masculinity and femininity (Orloff 1996: 51).

Changing our focus from sex to gender takes us from questions about how many women are in power, associated with debate about why there are so few, to questions about how we get more women into powerful positions, associated with debate about what difference it will make to have a greater presence of women amongst the powerful (Lovenduski 1998). In short, concern about the quantity of representation of women is *always* associated with considerations of what qualities are associated with women's participation in decision-making. Related to this is a danger that emphasis on women's formal decision-making roles may undervalue their roles in informal participatory democracy. Thus a further distinction is commonly made between *women's* political representation and participation and *feminist* representation and participation.

However there is considerable debate among feminists and other theorists about the causes, stability, results and implications of gender differences. Especially significant in this regard is the contention by many feminists that women should not seek equal presence to men in powerful positions because they will be 'incorporated' and changed by it, will become unable to represent women because they have been turned by male created institutions into political men. The counter-argument is that once a significant number and diversity of women occupy decision-making positions in institutions, the institutions will be transformed. The questions raised by these arguments are unavoidable in discussions of the political representation of women.

How do we understand changes in women's representation? What can be learned from experience in different countries?

The production of equality of women's representation is a long and complex process. Much of the acceleration of women's presence in Britain's representative bodies is part of a process that began in the nineteenth century, abated after 1928, and then re-emerged in the 1970s. Both a particular history and a continuous twenty to thirty year process of mobilization, intervention and debate in an array of representative institutions that includes political parties, women's organizations, democratic advocacy organizations, trade unions, and state policy machinery are behind changes in the 1980s and 1990s. Necessary to understanding the process are successive studies of activity in the interactive and evolving institutions in which representation takes place.

Experience abroad may bring about change at home. In France, for example, feminist experts repeatedly drew attention to the relatively low levels of the representation of women. Their work enabled feminist activists (sometimes the same people) to raise the issue over a twenty-year period, and eventually to 'constitutionalise' the right of women to be represented (Scott 1997, Lovecey 2000.) 'A Network of Experts on Decision-Making' funded by the European Commission brought the attention of feminist research to the Commission where femocrats attempted to insert statements claiming women's rights to representation into policy documents. The same strategy was pursued in the Council of Europe. Other examples include Italy, Britain, and international bodies such as the UN and the Commonwealth.

Feminist experts have an important role to play. The UN, for example, has made consistent use of feminist scholars employed as experts. This influence is amplified as the subunits of the UN Member States and other actors similarly seek advice. Feminist expertise is fed through a set of institutions and processes that inevitably dilute its content. It is nevertheless present and influential, central to the vision of change incorporated into UN documents and policy (*Beijing Platform for Action* 1995).

The influence of feminist expertise is reinforced by women's mobilization. Thousands of women wrote the global *Platform for Action* (*PfA*) agreed at Beijing in 1995, reflecting grass roots mobilizations in previous versions of UN policy. Later grass roots activities included mobilization around the *PfA*. The *PfA* calls for specific action by governments to increase the presence of women in all forms of decision-making. Policies should include mainstreaming and monitoring of women's interests and presence in order to plan for future action. In the area of women's representation two key strategic objectives are to be met. Measures must be taken to ensure women's equal access to and full participation in power structures and decision-making (UN strategic objective G1) and to increase women's capacity to participate in decision-making and leadership (UN strategic objective G2). The logic of the two strategic objectives is to increase demands for both women representatives (G1) and the supply of eligible women (G2) until a critical mass is reached. The strategic thinking is of an interactive process in which a new equilibrium of men's and women's representation should be achieved after which a substantial presence of both sexes in decision-making will seem natural and will be self-sustaining. Feminist influence in the formulation of the objectives and strategies outlined in the 178 pages of the *PfA* is clearly evident.

The monitoring of progress is a crucial component of equality policy, as true for political representation as it is for other areas of activity. In the case of the UN policy, the global implementation of the two objectives is far from straightforward. Different institutional, social and political arrangements offer different opportunities and barriers and therefore require different policies. Even within a reasonably 'uniform' region such as Western Europe there are patterns of increasing, decreasing and stagnant levels of women's presence in decision-making positions.

Studies of the political status of women postulate two political hierarchies, both of which are gendered. There is first a persistent and widespread pattern of decreasing numbers of women as decision-making hierarchies are ascended, and second, a functional division of labour between women and men whereby women are more likely to specialize in soft policy areas such as health, cultural affairs, education, social security, while men dominate the traditionally more prestigious areas of economic management, foreign affairs, defence and home affairs, which is apparent in most political elites.

Two opposing perspectives have been suggested to explain these divisions, both of which are 'testable' using time series data. On the one hand it is claimed that there is an 'iron law' of politics in which the proportions of women decrease as the hierarchy of power is ascended.[1] On the other hand it is argued that new mobilizations of voters take time to establish a presence in decision-making hierarchies. Known as the 'lag' hypothesis, this view posits that a pool of eligibles must become established at each level of a hierarchy before the next level can be ascended.[2] If the 'iron law' holds we would expect to see no change over time, while if the 'lag' hypothesis holds we would expect to see a steady increase of women in political elites wherever women are mobilized. That increase might stem from colonization by women of channels of recruitment such as political parties, and in turn lead to increased presences of women in other decision-making elites.

The concepts of supply and demand and the hypotheses of lags vs. iron laws of women's representation might be thought of as two related matrices that interact to produce different levels of women's representation.

	Supply	*Demand*
Lag	+	+
Iron Law	–	–

Where both supply and demand are increasing in a sector the lag hypothesis obtains (positive); where neither supply nor demand are increasing the iron law hypothesis obtains (negative); and where patterns of change in the supply of and demand for women decision-makers vary (mixed), outcomes are uncertain.

Such hypotheses are analytical constructs that afford useful ways of describing change and stagnation. They can be used to offer systematic accounts of progress at regular intervals. To drive improvements further they are often linked to the notion of critical mass, which is the level of women's presence required before differences are evident.[3]

Patterns of change in women's political representation should be examined 'in conjunction with everything else'. In modern politics, political representation takes place in a range of different councils, committees and social milieux that may not have the same significance in different political systems or at different times or for different political issues. Feminist research on women's political representation is concerned not only with how many women are present but also with who these women are, how they identify themselves, what they do, how they got there and what the institutions are like. Explaining the patterns of changing representation in elected assemblies is a major task that requires close knowledge of the 'public, institutionalized arrangement(s)', *qua* Pitkin, as well as a detailed knowledge of sex roles and gendered arrangements in the countries concerned. Not only does comparison offer analytic edge to our understanding of political change; it is also a useful *political* strategy. Exposing national differences in political representation 'problemetizes' poor levels of women's representation by drawing attention to it, action in one country may be proposed on the basis of practices that have proved successful in similar countries.

Indeed, as I have already suggested, events in other systems have frequently been part of the process of empowering women either through informal processes of diffusion of innovation or formally through the interventions of international organizations such as the UN, the Commonwealth and the Council of Europe, and supranational organizations such as the European Union.

The themes outlined above are the mainstay of discussions of women's political equality. They were repeatedly highlighted at Wilton Park, where the wide-ranging discussions of delegates repeatedly returned to issues of women's political representation.

Notes

1 Nina Cecile Raum, 'The political representation of women: a bird's eye view', in Lauri Karvonnen and Per Selle (eds), *Women in Nordic Politics: Closing the Gap.*

2 This is sometimes accompanied by the notion of shrinking institutions, discussed later in the paper. The shrinking institutions hypothesis claims that when women do ascend a political hierarchy into representative institutions it is an indication that the institutions have declined in importance.

3 In Dahlerup's (1988) examination of critical mass she specified that it was the level of women's presence necessary for critical acts to empower women to be made.

2 The role of Parliamentarians[1]

> In all Commonwealth societies women are suppressed. Our continuing failure to genuinely respond to the challenge of attaining human equality is demonstrated by the very composition of our meeting. We need only to look at the group gathered here to see that maleness is a prerequisite for political leadership. It cannot be that we pride ourselves when this special collective distinguishes itself by defining women as alien beings.[2]

The issue of the political representation of women has become a central part of the contemporary political agenda. Driven by advocates of women's rights and proponents of representative democracy, women's representation has been taken up by political parties, national governments, NGOs and established international organizations including, inter alia, the Commonwealth, the United Nations, the Council of Europe and the European Union. The Commonwealth Parliamentary Association is an important actor in this process, offering both institutional support and policy frameworks to its members. Commonwealth Parliamentary Association (CPA) policy and strategy might be understood as answers to the question 'what should and can Parliamentarians do to empower women?'

It is not only at Head of State Level that Commonwealth women are absent. In the year 2000, of the 8306 seats in the national Parliaments of the Commonwealth, 1145 (13.8 per cent) were occupied by women. Although this is more than the world average of 13.1 per cent, it is nowhere near the 30 per cent target set by the Commonwealth Heads of Government Meeting (CHOGM) in Edinburgh in 1997[3] and confirmed at the Sixth Meeting of Commonwealth Ministers Responsible for Women's Affairs in New Delhi in 2000.[4]

The pattern of women's representation in the Commonwealth is not uniform. In the Pacific and Asian regions, excluding Australia, 8.6 per cent and 8.7 per cent of parliamentary seats are held by women. In Australia and Canada the figures are 25 per cent and 22.5 per cent. Only South Africa (30.3 per cent) and New Zealand (30.8 per cent) have reached the 30 per cent target set for 2005. Although the less powerful upper houses in Barbados (33.3 per cent), Bahamas (31.3 per cent), Belize (44.4 per cent) and Trinidad and Tobago (32.3 per cent) have all met the target, their lower chambers fall well short of 30 per cent. The figures for lower chambers are: Barbados (10.7 per cent), Bahamas (15 per cent), and Belize (6.9 per cent) and Trinidad and Tobago (10.8 per cent).[5]

When the data are extended to include the entire national, state, provincial and territorial parliaments of the Commonwealth Parliamentary Association (CPA) the overall percentage falls to 12.3 per cent. Amongst these subassemblies are Gauteng (34.2 per cent), North-West Provincial Legislature (33.3 per cent), Falkland Islands Legislative Council (30 per cent), the Scottish Assembly (37 per cent) and the Welsh Assembly (40 per cent).

The mixed pattern of women's share of legislative seats raises interesting questions about why women are under-represented, about what kind of practices and activities are best suited to increase women's presence in public life and about what is being done to improve women's presence. The Commonwealth Parliamentary Association and Commonwealth Women Parliamentarians (CWP) have played an active part in developing policies to enhance women's access. The CPA recognizes that women's rights require improved representation in Parliament and for women Parliamentarians in the CPA.

Within the CPA the CWP is the main institutional device for recognizing and treating issues of sex equality and women's concerns. The aims of the CWP are to further the representation of women in Parliament throughout the Commonwealth and to ensure that matters of concern to women are brought to the attention of the CPA, as well as in individual parliaments. Established in 1989 and guided by a sixteen-member Steering Committee, the CWP is an important resource for Commonwealth women Parliamentarians. Since its establishment there has been an increase of women's participation in the CPA and gender-equality has become an overtly stated aim of the Association. CWP meetings are held during annual Commonwealth Parliamentary Conferences. The meetings provide a focal point for women Parliamentarians to meet and network. This is facilitated by a computerized roster of biographical data on women members of the Commonwealth kept by the CPA. In 1995, CWP meetings became part of the normal conference programme, and an integral part of the conference with input into the programme of the conference. Thus, in 1999 delegates debated the use of quotas and in 2000 they considered how parliamentary practice can be modified to remove barriers to the political, economic and social development of women.[6] In addition the CWP can propose topics for CPA study groups and special conferences (such as the Wilton Park Conference on which this book is based). At its meeting in Cyprus in October 1993 the CWP set up a Task Force to investigate and prepare a report into the barriers to women's full participation in Parliament. The CPA has also assisted the Gender Affairs Department of the Commonwealth Secretariat in a series of regional symposia, designed to increase women's representation in political decision-making and peace processes at the highest levels, and aims to promote a gender-sensitive approach to political decision-making and conflict prevention.

What are the contributions to women's representation that might be made by Parliamentarians? Four kinds of effect have been important:

- making an impact on the legislature
- tackling the root causes of gender inequality
- working in political parties
- reforming the parliaments.

Making an Impact on the Legislature

Individuals can use parliamentary resources and opportunities to promote women's equality. For example, they may intervene in debate to extend the policy agenda to matters previously conceived of as 'domestic'. Through such processes violence against women has come to be seen as a legitimate area of public concern, an appropriate area for legislative action. There are many examples of such activity. Acting as individual MPs, women MPs in India introduced private Bills such as the Married Women (Protection of Rights) Bill, 1990, the Prohibition of Test for Pre-Birth Sex Determination Bill, 1987, and the Promotion of Casteless and Religionless Society Bill, 1982. Private Bills are not often successful, but they are published, they contribute to debate, they attract the attention of the press and they may serve as catalysts for government action on an issue.[7] Women MPs in the Cook Islands instigated the Matrimonial Property Act 1991–2, a law that protects the land rights of Cook Island women married to foreigners and provides for the equal distribution of property between spouses when their marriage ends.[8]

Working together, women MPs can be more effective. Many Commonwealth parliaments have parliamentary party women's sections and some (South Africa, Zambia, Malawi, Botswana and Tanzania) have all-party or cross-party women's groups. In the case of Tanzania the Women's parliamentary group is modelled on the CWP international women's caucus. Local branches of the CWP supplement parliamentary activity and enable women MPs to meet together (irrespective of party membership) to discuss the gender impact of legislation and develop strategies to be more effective in Parliament. Such groups may produce significant organizational and institutional innovation. For example the Malaysian local chapter of the CWP set up in 1993 to act as an informal lobby group on issues of concern to women, came to play an important part in setting up the Muslim Parliamentarians group involving over thirty Muslim countries.[9]

Tackling the Root Causes of Gender Inequality

Gender inequality is often a manifestation of other forms of inequality such as poverty, class, caste and ethnic divisions and so forth. Dealing with such issues is part of the work of any modern legislature. Adequate and gender-sensitive treatment of these issues should improve women's inequality. An example is the introduction of Minimum Wage legislation in Britain. This measure contributed to the first diminution of the pay gap between women and men since the 1970s. But to get to the stage where such measures might be introduced in a gender-sensitive manner, attitudes and ideas about sex roles need to be changed. For example, development programmes for children have been designed to expose them to knowledge about political and parliamentary processes. Such programmes promote political careers for both boys and girls. The CPA uses Commonwealth Day as an opportunity to introduce young people to the significance and value of the Commonwealth and of parliamentary democracy. Politicians should be encouraged to talk to students and others about parliamentary democracy, and use the CPA and such occasions as Commonwealth Day as opportunities to do so. They should pay particular attention to initiatives aimed at young women. Women Parliamentarians are important role models for younger women. A number of initiatives have been taken, with due attention to sex equality, to bring more young people into parliamentary politics. The New Brunswick Legislature initiated a Student Legislative Seminar, a non-partisan programme intended to provide equal numbers of boys and girls with a better understanding of government. The CPA plans a sex-balanced Millennium Youth Parliament this year.

Working in Political Parties

Political parties are the vital channels of recruitment into public office in parliamentary democracies. It is parties that have the major say in who candidates are, how they are selected and what their qualifications should be. Thus when trying to explain low levels of women's political representation, it is vital to consider the roles of political parties. Often parties play a contradictory role. At the same time as they attempt, at least formally, to promote women politicians, they operate in confrontational and aggressive ways which are known to deter more women than men. In systems in which party discipline is strong, and partisan loyalty is de rigueur, parties may limit the ability of political women, especially parliamentary women to come together. Therefore the formal activities of parties that are designed to promote women's access to parliamentary careers need to be assessed in the light of the informal practices and customs that may be very inhibiting. At the same time the initiatives should be welcomed. Examples include training programmes for potential women candidates in Canada (all parties), the UK (Labour Party), written materials encouraging women to run for political office (New Zealand

Labour Party, all UK parties) and the facilitation of party women's networks by established women's officers, conferences and so on.

Reforming the Parliaments

Finally, parliaments themselves need to be scrutinized for their women-friendliness. When Nancy Astor, the first British woman MP, took her seat in the House of Commons, her male colleagues went out of their way to embarrass her. Her experiences became all too common. Not only did future British women MPs have to endure similar treatment, but also women across the Commonwealth have had to struggle with parliamentary practices that were designed by and for men. Adversarial styles of debate, brutal working hours, the absence of crèches and even the absence of women's lavatories served to alienate women, to reduce their effectiveness and to emphasize their status as 'outsiders'.

Many parliaments have standing orders that encourage adversarial behaviour, and even their seating arrangements emphasize conflict. In recent years, attempts to produce reforms of these practices have been made by new parliaments set up to include women from the outset. In South Africa session times were changed, a crèche established and rules governing attire were changed because of the influence of women members. In Scotland and Wales attempts were made to build women-friendliness into the procedures from the outset (see chapter 3).

In conclusion, increasing the number of women Parliamentarians will not happen naturally. Specific programmes would be needed to rectify the democratic deficit that currently exists in the Commonwealth. Work on this has begun in most Commonwealth countries, but the process will take time and will involve a transformation of existing relationships and institutions.

Discussion

Institutions including parliaments, political parties, NGOs and international organizations all have a part to play in improving the representation of women. Different systems experience different problems but some of the barriers to women are generally present in most systems. Commonwealth experience suggests a number of strategies that might prove effective in improving women's political representation.

Particular and General Problems and Difficulties

1. The problem in Kuwait is most severe. Women are still legally prevented from entering the Legislature.
2. Fundamental change in society is difficult and slow.
3. It was frequently stated in the discussion that women dislike politics.
4. NGOs do not do enough in this area.
5. Politics is seen to be incompatible with women's roles.

Causes of Women's Under-representation

1. The ambivalence of women who are reluctant to participate in politics for various reasons including their attachment to their traditional roles and the masculinity of political life.
2. Failure by political parties to nominate women candidates for winnable seats.
3. The aggressive nature of the party system encourages women to oppose each other, limiting their ability to be effective as women.
4. Resistance by male politicians who may be ambivalent about women politicians and who do not wish to change existing parliamentary arrangements. For example, prior to 1978 the Nova Scotia Legislature never had more than a single woman representative, and it had no facilities for the three women elected in 1981.
5. Grass roots women's activities often do not filter through to Parliament. For example, Caribbean women are very active at local level, but only poorly represented in legislatures.

Strategies to Improve Women's Political Representation

1. Different levels of development require different approaches. The nature and strength of the barriers to political participation vary by country, culture and political system.
2. Elect more women. This may sound circular but once women are there in sufficient numbers they change the atmosphere and create an environment that is more supportive of women. This is shown by the South African experience, and in New Zealand and Scotland.

3. Role models are important, and leadership from women is necessary for progress to be made.
4. Parliamentarians themselves can make a big difference. Both men and women, acting as individuals or in groups, caucuses and so on, can have an impact both on the political agenda and on the way issues are discussed and understood in gendered terms.
5. All-party groups are especially effective. Politics is a continuous process into which women's representation issues need to be integrated.
6. Legislation can both lead and follow opinion. The opinion forming capacities of legislation should be used to reproduce laws that will change social attitudes about gender.
7. Education and training workshops have a massive effect on women's political ambitions. These need to be well funded.
8. Parliamentary women need to cultivate and stay close to grass roots women.
9. Mentoring programmes and childcare facilities in elected assemblies are helpful.
10. The cause of women's representation needs the support of male politicians. It is important to mobilize the sympathy many male politicians have for women's rights.
11. Electoral systems have differing effects on representation. Appropriate electoral systems should be chosen.

Notes

1 Based on the presentation by Arthur Donahoe, QC and Secretary-General, Commonwealth Parliamentary Association.
2 President Mbeki, Opening Address at the Commonwealth Heads of Government Meeting. Durban, South Africa, 12 November 1999.
3 Commonwealth Edinburgh Communiqué 1997.
4 New Delhi 16–19 April 2000. Commonwealth Secretariat Website www.thecommonwealth.org.
5 www.ipu.org. Accessed 18 June 2000.
6 Conference held in London on 22 September 2000.
7 C.K. Jain (1993) *Women Parliamentarians in India*. Lok Sabha.
8 Information provided by Hon. Ngamu Munokoa, MP Cook Islands.
9 'Priorities for women in politics', *The Parliamentarian*, October 1996.

3 Representation without the incumbency barrier: the example of Scotland[1]

The election of a critical mass of women to the Scottish Parliament has attracted worldwide attention, as has the determination to make the Scottish Parliament a woman-friendly legislature. From 6 May 1999 when the first elections for the Scottish Parliament were held, progress toward balanced political representation in Scotland has been impressive.

- 48 per cent of the newly elected MSPs are women.
- Equal opportunity is a central operating principle of the Standing Orders and Procedures of the new Parliament.
- Five of the Ministers in the new government are women (23 per cent).
- Women chair six of the sixteen parliamentary committees
- Sixty-seven women (37.5 per cent) and ninety-three men (62.5 per cent) are members of parliamentary committees (multiple memberships).
- A cross-cutting Equal Opportunities Committee has been established in the Parliament.
- An Equality Unit has been established in the Scottish Executive.
- Mainstreaming of equalities is required to be integrated into the policies and practices of the Parliament and the Executive.

What are the lessons of the Scottish achievement? What mechanisms are most effective at increasing the representation of women in parliaments? How is the effectiveness of women Parliamentarians best maximized? Increasing the political representation of women is a matter of operating in particular contexts of nation, locality and culture. This point is well illustrated by the contrasting examples of Scotland and Malaysia (to be discussed in chapter 12).

Incumbency effects are widely believed to be one of the greatest barriers to women's political representation. Except where term limits obtain, the convention is that Parliamentarians continue to stand for a parliamentary seat once they have won it, hence safe seats tend to remain in the same (male) control for the course of a political career. The new assemblies established in Scotland and Wales in 1999 therefore offered a significant opportunity for political parties to demonstrate their commitments to women's representation. There were no incumbents to be displaced in order to achieve balanced representation. The results were striking. At parliamentary level, Scotland is one of the countries that are comfortably above the Commonwealth target of 30 per cent of women at decision-making levels in the public and private sector. At other levels women's representation is below the target, but success in Parliament offers a model and process that is likely to be used throughout the system. The portfolios held by women members of the executive are significant. They include health, communities and transport.

Responsibilities for equality issues are threaded through the Standing Orders and Procedures of the Parliament. The Ministerial team is committed to equality between men and women and held accountable for this commitment by the full array of parliamentary mechanisms. Sixteen legislative committees scrutinize legislation and hold the executive to account. All have responsibilities for equality and one committee deals exclusively with equality issues and equal opportunities. Equal opportunities is one of the four founding principles of the Scottish Parliament, endorsed by its members. Working practices have been designed to enable women's participation (see below). These arrangements did not simply happen, nor may they be taken for granted. They were the result of a long campaign and are the objects of a continuing struggle in which women's advocates are mobilized to secure equality of representation and a women-friendly political environment in Scotland.

It's a Process: the Political Parties

The election of a critical mass of women MSPs was based on the involvement of women in civic life and their mobilization within the political parties, especially the Scottish Labour Party. The process that led to the establishment of the Parliament, and particularly the selection of candidates, was fraught with difficulty. The Labour Party in Scotland and in Wales provided opportunities and encouragement to get women onto the political platform. That is a first step, once on the platform it is necessary to ensure that women's voices are heard, a lesson reinforced by the experience of women in the House of Commons. According to Jackie Baillie, Labour women at Westminster have only recently started to voice their concerns. The election of 101 Labour women MPs in May 1997 began a process of change in the democratic make-up of British political institutions. This process was carried through to the programme of devolution in Scotland and Wales. A significant and lengthy set of debates and negations paved the way. Prior to the 1997 election the Liberal Democrats and the Labour Party in Scotland signed a voluntary agreement to ensure that equal numbers of men and women were elected to Parliament. Labour translated this commitment into positive action, opting for a voluntary system to be implemented with the political parties rather than a mandatory legislative quota of the kind that is found in Belgium. Among the political parties in Scotland, only Labour adopted specific mechanisms to ensure gender balance in the party group in the legislature. Other parties considered and debated the use of a mechanism, but for various reasons did not adopt one.

The electoral system adopted in Scotland is the additional member system. According to this system there are two electoral routes to Parliament, via a constituency seat or via a list seat. The electorate has two votes each, one for the constituency member of their choice and one for the political party of their choice. The individual vote works in the same way as that for the House of Commons. The party vote is based on eight regions and is used to level out the disproportion in party support that sometimes arises from a system wholly based on single member constituencies.

'Twinning' was the term coined to describe the process by which Labour secured 50 per cent representation of women on Labour benches. The Labour Party of Scotland recognized that most of its seats would be obtained in the constituency elections rather than from the list elections, hence a woman's representation mechanism had to be designed that was effective for the constituency seats. Making fair selection mechanisms for such seats is very difficult. After much discussion and planning a scheme was designed to 'twin' constituencies to allow both men and women to stand for election. Under this scheme, constituency seats were paired on the basis of winnability and other characteristics for the purposes of candidate selection. In each pair of seats, the woman with the highest number of votes was selected as the Labour candidate for one of the constituencies at the same time as the man with the highest number of votes was selected as the Labour candidate for the other. This mechanism was used to select Labour candidates for all constituencies with the exception of the four Highlands and Islands constituencies.

To the observer, the twinning system must seem very elaborate. However it worked. It avoided the attention of the courts and it successfully returned twenty-eight Labour women and twenty-eight Labour men to the Parliament. Other parties were less successful. The SNP followed with 43 per cent women MSPs, and the Conservatives and Liberals trailed well behind with 17 per cent and 12 per cent respectively.

The overall result therefore shows that even in a new Parliament, with no incumbency barriers, the equal representation of women cannot be taken for granted. It requires political will within the parties. Labour is justifiably proud of its results in Scotland, but it is important to realize that its commitments would not have been made without sustained pressure for change from women's organizations, trade unions and the women in the Labour party. Moreover, there was considerable resistance to 'twinning'. Opponents trotted out the standard and well-worn excuses. 'Not enough women of quality are available', 'it is against employment law' and 'it's discriminatory' were all frequently intoned by opponents.

The Parliament: Links with Women

The process in the political parties was not the end of the matter. Not only does the debate over women's representation continue inside the parties, but it also became a part of the newly created institutions. The Parliament has provided a new focus for democracy in Scotland. It is committed to policy making that is open, participative and consultative. MSPs are anxious to help communities find a voice on matters that concern them. Within this process, active encouragement is given to the inclusion of women.

The Parliament established a Civic Forum within which women are represented. The Women in Scotland Consultative Forum of 700 women's organizations was established in 1997 and meets at least twice a year. Chaired by MSP Jackie Baillie, forum meetings enable officials and Ministers from across the Scottish Executive to engage directly with women on subjects that are chosen by the women themselves. Reports are produced after each meeting and action points are circulated to policy divisions within the executive. For example, the May 2000 meeting of the Women's Forum discussed training, the economy and social inclusion. The forum gives women the opportunity to contribute directly to policy making, ensures that their voices are heard and that their concerns are listened to.

Through various mechanisms the Scottish Parliament has acquired a growing understanding of women's concerns. Important initiatives have been taken to address poverty in a programme that also addresses issues of childcare and other children's concerns, women's health, violence to women, women's employment and women's shares of public appointments.

Poverty

Women are more likely to experience and to live in conditions of poverty than are men. Poverty is not simply about income and money it is also about health, education, housing and employment. Poverty eats away at the hopes of those who experience it and gives rise to a poverty of expectation that is passed down from one generation to the next. Experience worldwide shows that these are not problems that will be solved overnight. The response of the Scottish Parliament therefore has been to set in motion a twenty-year programme designed to tackle poverty and to regenerate the country's most disadvantaged communities. A good start has been made. Since 1997 long-term youth unemployment fell by 71 per cent, long-term unemployment overall fell by 53 per cent. It is expected that 100 000 Scottish children will be lifted out of poverty by 2002. In short the early signs of programme accomplishments are positive.

Women are at the heart of the poverty programme within which promoting greater equality is a central goal.

Children

Education policy should ensure that girls and boys have the same access to education. Childcare provision is made in the form of nursery places for all four-year-olds. By the end of the Parliament provision will also be available for all three-year-olds. A freephone information helpline has been established on childcare issues.

Health

Women's health is adversely affected by poverty, stress, domestic abuse and overwork. The executive is looking at health initiatives in the broad areas of life circumstances, lifestyles and priority health objectives.

Violence

Physical and sexual abuse affects women in all societies. The trauma affects their mental health and the wellbeing of their children. Accordingly, tackling domestic violence is a priority in Scotland. A Domestic Abuse Service Development Fund worth £8 million opened on 1 April 2000, to provide services across Scotland. Further measures will include the strengthening of protection law and work to change attitudes.

Work and Employment

Full participation in the Labour market is a prerequisite to women's equality. In Scotland, £1 million has been set aside to extend micro credit to the whole of the Scottish Enterprise Network.

Public Appointments

The Scottish Executive is concerned to improve women's share of Public Appointments and has completed a process of consultation about how to open the procedures so that a better gender balance is achieved. Equal Opportunities are established within the Executive and within the Parliament. The policy of gender mainstreaming will operate across the whole of government policy development, legislation and service delivery.

Elected Women

The Scottish Parliament will also play a part in encouraging women to stand for election, and has put in place a pattern of working practices that suits women and family life. Sessions closely mirror school terms and there are no late night sittings. However, there is still room for improvement, particularly for those MSPs who live out of daily travelling distance from the Parliament in Edinburgh.

Men

The media often reflect the treatment of women and women's issues by men. In the political arena the way that men respond to women MSPs and the issues they raise is often reflected in media stories. Too many men still aim to enhance their own standing by undermining and unfairly criticizing the women around them. The backlash that this generates can be very damaging, and women need to be alert to it and at the same time to cultivate beneficial relationships with the media.

The Labour Party's selection process in Scotland did the job it was meant to do, delivering gender balance and bringing women into the new Parliament. Now attention has turned to the behaviour and achievements of those who are on the political stage. Everyone understands that the stakes are very high.

Discussion

There is no cause for complacency. The high proportions of women in the Parliament are not reflected in other levels of the system. For example, women form only 22 per cent of councillors in Scotland and well under 30 per cent of the Scottish Executive. The goal of gender balance must be kept on the political agenda and there is a need to ensure that all the political parties take steps to improve women's representation. Informal arrangements may not be enough to keep policies of gender equality on target; hence policy makers should consider formal, legislative mechanisms. Quotas on the same lines as are found in the Nordic states should govern public appointments. Such quotas should include the cabinet and the parliamentary committees and offices.

Note

1 Based on the presentation by the Hon. Jackie Baillie MSP.

4 Waving goodbye to dinosaurs: the Northern Ireland Women's Coalition[1]

As far as history goes
We were never
At the scene of the crime[2]

'But we were in the neighbourhood', said Monica McWilliams, a delegate to the Stormont Peace Negotiations from the Northern Ireland Women's Coalition (NIWC) as she considered how women's groups could contribute to the resolution of conflict. Using the language of feminist theory she described her experiences and outlined the structure of women's organizations in Northern Ireland. In the course of affirming the need for reconciliation in Northern Ireland she generalized about the effects of fear and sectarianism on the political community and offered her observations on how to transcend those effects. She argued that the normal strategies and skills of women were good strategies and skills with which to rebuild political community.

Monica McWilliams and Pearl Sagar were two NIWC women at the Stormont peace negotiations. Other negotiators regarded them as a 'double other' because they were women and because they each came from a different political and religious background, yet worked together. They disrupted the status quo because they were women and because they co-operated with each other despite political and religious differences. The initial reaction to their efforts was a serious attempt to subordinate the two women, to make them objects of political derision, to silence them. McWilliams attributed this to the effects of fear. The protagonists read the attempts made by the Women's Coalition to create a consensus style of politics and focus on the need for honourable compromise as a demand for surrender rather than as a honourable compromise.

Yet, said McWilliams, 'whilst acting out of fear is natural, acting from hope is brave'. Hope is necessary to reconciliation. Reconciliation matters because it creates a common space into which everyone can move. Without that space division and separation are normalized and integration becomes impossible. What Northern Ireland needs is integration. Real integration will only come from genuine engagement in political dialogue. The common space created by the peace process cannot be taken for granted; if it is not occupied by different, but recognized voices, it will disappear.

In other words, the quest for commonality, something well understood by women, will succeed only if it registers and respects difference. The women who were community activists throughout the conflict know that finding common ground is a dynamic process through which understandings are broadened and change is possible. Coming from the background of women's activism the Women's Coalition members struggled to offer not only their own personal experiences of resistance to harassment, but also their ability to conceptualize their experiences and build the coalitions that are necessary to reconciliation. A key strategy is 'rooting and shifting'. Each woman brings her roots with her in the form of her own membership and identity. At the same time each woman tries to shift and to put herself in an exchange with women who have a different situation and identity. Shifting is not an abandonment of identity, values or aspirations. It does, however, demand that one is open to change and development as a result of the contact with others with divergent views. In this language reconciliation is a process, incomplete and ongoing. It is a set of activities in which the 'other' is engaged and a changing world is accepted in a spirit of openness. Its aim is to heal division, to articulate common purposes and expand horizons. On the last night of the Northern Ireland Peace negotiations the Women's Coalition delegates convinced the participants to insert the right of women to equal participation into the Good Friday Agreement.

According to McWilliams' account, women have been the agents of peace in Northern Ireland for more than twenty years.

There are over 1200 registered women's organizations in Northern Ireland. They were at the heart of civil disobedience and ran campaigns for housing, employment and voting. They carried a placard demanding 'one man, one vote' as well as organizing to establish women's centres, rape crisis and Women's Aid networks. When politicians did not respond, women bypassed them, often establishing their own services. This was subversive. Active, but politically homeless women were a direct challenge to the institutions of representative democracy. The Women's Coalition drew on a network built up over twenty-five years of struggle and working across divisions in the community. They were networked globally with links to Guatemalan, South African and Indian women.

However they were not initially accepted as legitimate participants in the peace process. When the Stormont negotiations began the women were congratulated on their work, but not invited to participate. They contacted Whitehall in protest, held meetings all over the country and contacted all of the women's groups. Some were fearful of entering the political mainstream, feeling that it might jeopardize their efficient and productive work as outsiders. They demanded an inclusionary system calling for the implementation of the Beijing platform. Women's rights were presented as human rights. Politicians claimed they could not find suitable women. In response, however, women made the most of the rules of the political game. Where a Republican issue appeared to be in question, Unionist women were used to demonstrate that women were prepared to stand for election and speak for the community. Suddenly the politicians were able to find women willing to be candidates. In this way the NIWC went from being regarded as an interesting phenomena that would go away to an electable organization, represented in the negotiations.

The significance of the negotiations was to be found as much in the process as in the outcome. The NIWC argued strongly for the voting system used in South Africa, a system built on consensus rather than majority voting. Anything proposed therefore had to stand up in both communities. A Civic Forum has been established to ensure the inclusion of organizations of all kinds. A new equality commission has been set up to ensure that all policies are assessed for fair treatment. In Northern Ireland dealing with the truth had resonance with the knowledge gained from working with domestic violence survivors who want to hear acknowledgement and the taking of responsibility. The women showed that working with adversaries is not surrender but giving difference its due. The lessons of the experiences were sometimes prosaic, but always important. Women showed how humiliation could be resisted by getting support, using humour and naming and shaming.

Discussion

Monica McWilliams is a role model, inspirational and exceptional. Her experience shows how women can make a difference to politics without acting like men. The political roles of women were continuously remade. In the wake of the peace process the NIWC are following the implementation of the treaty. They are also building coalitions with men, for example fathers who want to be with their children, and working on such issues as domestic violence. Their experience before, during and since the process offers important lessons for women's political action. Even under very difficult circumstances at least five operating rules apply:

1. Women can push through women's issues by networking with other groups, organizations and parties.
2. Women's rights are human rights and women have an interest in human rights. However, it is important to be able to generalize from women's issues to community issues, but
3. Nevertheless, women's experience on women's issues has application to all issues. Survivors on self-help projects befriend each other and become part of the coalition.
4. When women are not invited to the negotiating table, they must insist on being invited.
5. It is important to build coalitions with men who are fathers, husbands and victims.

Notes

1 Professor Monica McWilliams, Delegate, Stormont Peace Negotiations, Northern Ireland Women's Coalition, Belfast.
2 Evan Boland *It's a Women's World.*

5 Making Parliamentarians listen to women voters and getting women elected[1]

Making Parliament Listen

In the UK getting Parliamentarians to listen at all is something of a challenge. Parliament and politics are verbal activities. Political institutions are designed so that politicians are typically judged by how well they can talk, not how well they listen. The 'Parle' in Parliament means talk. To become an MP candidates must perform talk; they make a speech at their selection conference and answer questions in public. The talking however is not necessarily popular. In the UK voters, especially women voters, frequently report that they think Parliament is just a talking shop.

Their perceptions are guided by the media, but often founded on misperceptions about what Parliament is for and how it works. Knowledge of the role of Parliament and its relationship with the Executive is not widely held and often confused and mistaken. But it is not only lack of voter civic education that produces imperfect perceptions of Parliament. MPs contribute to the problem by their tendency to be long-winded and repetitive when they talk. Long-windedness is rewarded in the House of Commons where the main weapon of the current opposition is the filibuster, the long speech or series of speeches that prevents a vote from being taken and delays or prevents a policy from being adopted.

Sheilagh Diplock's view is that women MPs are less patient with long and pointless speechifying, but not immune to it themselves. In the current House of Commons there is evidence of a desire for change. MPs and peers from all parties are weary of a barren opposition strategy. They see the current operation of the house as a waste of time and want to be either in the Government or in their constituencies 'helping' their constituents.

The new legislatures in Scotland and Wales offer a contrast for two reasons. First, elected under a new electoral system for Britain (the additional member system), neither has a party with an overall majority. The Scottish Executive is a coalition of parties and the Welsh Assembly has a minority Executive. The first Welsh leader paid insufficient attention to his minority status and was voted out, and replaced by a more consensual leader with a more inclusive style. Second, both legislatures are built around standing orders designed, in part, to avoid the worst practices of the House of Commons. They augur a new and more modern style of parliamentary work and suggest that listening may become more important in the future.

Although they are talkers rather than listeners, MPs do see the need to listen to voters. Most agree that the previous Conservative Government lost the 1997 election because it was out of touch with the voters. New Labour MPs have been instructed to spend time in their constituencies listening to voters. The new communications technologies mean that former reliance on the MP's postbag as an indicator of public opinion is being replaced by other ways of listening.

Women and Listening

Politicians may not be not good listeners, but neither are women good at making themselves heard. This is often not because of any problem women have about speaking; it is rather a matter of how men respond to women's voices in the public arena. One of the most popular Fawcett Society cartoons from the Fawcett Funny Girls exhibition was of a meeting room containing five men and one woman. The caption was the chair of the meeting saying, 'That is a good suggestion, Miss Trigg. Perhaps one of the men would like to make it.' Again and again women report experience of this situation. Because politicians are mainly men, women face a double barrier in making themselves heard, the barrier of the not listening politician and the barrier of the not hearing man.

To take the discussion further, it is necessary to distinguish between the behaviour of politicians during election campaigns and their behaviour 'between' elections.

Elections

Traditionally elections were the time at which voters communicated their wishes and demands to politicians. Until recently the relationship between voters and elected MPs was distant. The Burkean tradition of British politics held that the elected MP was not a delegate but a representative who would think, deliberate, and make wise decisions in the common interest. Report back time was the next election. The Burkean model held for most of the nineteenth and early twentieth centuries, giving way to a more responsive mode only in recent years.

In contemporary British politics the manifesto of the competing and winning parties is more central. Voters are thought to listen to and read the policy platforms of the candidates. Once elected, voters expect candidates to meet the commitments they make in the manifesto. One product of this kind of accountability is that manifestos tend to promise less than once they did. For the 1997 general election Labour summarized its manifesto in only five pledges that it promised to implement, because its research had told it that voters were fed up with politicians who promised much and delivered little. Although the Labour Party had a manifesto, it built its campaign around five fairly specific pledges.

Whatever their shortcomings, elections offer the best opportunity to get politicians to take notice of women. In recent years, women's organizations and advocates have learned how to make the most of this opportunity. The Fawcett Society, for example, ran a very successful 'Listen to my Vote' campaign in 1997. Feminist advocates made full use of the gender gap in voting whereby women were less likely than men to vote Labour and more likely than men to be floating voters, making their decisions much later in the campaign. That work continues. A recent Fabian pamphlet by Harriet Harman (with research from Deborah Mattinson) pursues the gender gap theme. The gender gap was partly closed by Labour in 1997, but recent polls show that it has reopened. This gender gap in a universe of falling voter loyalties enables women's advocates to get the attention of politicians who cannot win elections without women's votes. Traditionally the Conservatives relied on women's votes; today women voters are more attentive to policy pledges and more likely to shop around in the electoral marketplace.

Between Elections

Between elections, the difficulties of getting politicians to listen are much greater. However, despite its huge majority, the current UK Government is not confident; it pays close attention to voter opinion, using a raft of devices to tune into it. Focus groups, polling, a listening to women tour, a people's panel, questionnaires on specific policy and UK Online, all are used to find out what voters think of the Government, and within that, what women distinctly think.

The Government's approach has been widely criticized, mainly for being too superficial. Many critics say that the Government uses the information it gets in this way not to redirect policy, but only to improve presentation – 'spin'. The close attention the Government pays to how it communicates what it is doing to voters, especially women, is one of its most notable features. However, research by Deborah Mattinson of Opinion Research International points to a feature of women voters that render the Government's efforts wasted. Women judge policy success or failure by their own experience. They want to see tangible improvements. They make their judgements on the basis of whether their children, granny, partner are getting better education, better health care, better employment prospects and conditions. They are unimpressed by statistics. The frequent and confusing announcements of increased spending on one priority or another do little for them; they want to see results on the ground. The sophisticated presentations of 'spin' are counterproductive when nothing else is changing.

A further complication of the 'listening to people' style of government is that it bypasses Parliament, producing complaints from MPs that they are being sidelined and raising important constitutional questions about accountability and representation. Opportunities to listen in this way continue to increase. The online revolution is having a considerable effect on politics. The Hansard Society is running a pilot scheme of online consultations between

Parliamentarians and groups of voters. Among these was a highly successful consultation between MPs and survivors of domestic violence. The online forum offered a safe place for survivors to answer MPs' questions and tell their stories. Many women were using the technology for the first time. The lessons from the pilot were published in a report on social inclusion and the Internet (Coleman and Normann, 2000). The real explosion in ICT technology is still to come with digital TV, WAP phones and other innovations. The Hansard Society, working with British Telecom, is to develop a virtual MP's office to demonstrate how new technology can enhance communications between constituents and MPs. Such devices may overcome the problems of time and distance that have impeded women more than men from political participation and might get women's voices heard closer to the centre of power. To take full advantage however, women must be organized and ready to lead the new democratic revolution.

The Hansard Society is an example of a long-standing non-party organization. Its formal interest is in the study of Parliament. Recently it has become aware of issues of women's political representation and made significant efforts to press women's claims. Such concern by an interest group became more common in Britain in the 1990s. In the 1980s however, interest groups were rarely concerned about women's representation, a gap that was partly filled by the foundation of the 300 Group.

Getting Women Elected: The 300 Group

The 300 group, an all-party women's pressure group, was founded by Lesley Abdela and others after the 1979 General Election to bring more women into elected office. It drew its approach from marketing strategy. The aim was to create demand for women politicians by use of publicity, and to affect the supply of women by encouraging and enabling them to seek elected office at local or national level. Supply would then impact on demand because aspirant women politicians would be seen as good products.

To enable women to become skilled participants the 300 group, in conjunction with *Cosmopolitan* magazine, offered training days. These sessions trained women in the political skills of speaking in public, of debating, writing press releases and so forth. Training was also given in understanding the political processes. Thus women were informed about the regimes for candidate selection, about the working of the House of Commons and local councils and about the economy, the budgetary process, foreign policy, the European Communities and other issue areas.

British political parties and trade unions now routinely provide such training. Similar programmes are offered in the Bahamas, in Bangladesh, Vietnam, Saint Lucia, India, Belize, Papua New Guinea and Switzerland. Either publicity or training or both may originate in political parties, trade unions and women's organizations and networks. No examples were offered of instances where governments offered training.

Note

1 Based on contributions from Sheilagh Diplock and Lesley Abdela.

6 The Beijing process[1]

The Beijing process is the most recent and comprehensive manifestation of the UN attempt to facilitate sex equality. Since 1975, an international meeting of national spokespersons on women's rights has taken place every ten years. Since the first meeting in Mexico City in 1975, the official meeting has been accompanied by unofficial meetings of all kinds, mainly organized by NGOs. NGOs also have input into the official meetings. Thousands of women contribute to the process. In 1995 the meeting at Beijing adopted a document (*Platform for Action, PfA*) setting out commitments to women's rights, with the intention that member states would agree to it. The *PfA* attempts to implement the UN Convention on Discrimination Against Women (CEDAW) and accordingly commits members to improvements in twelve core areas:

- poverty
- education and training
- health
- violence
- armed conflict
- the economy
- power and decision-making
- institutional mechanisms for the advancement of women
- human rights
- the media
- the environment
- the girl child.

Unlike the CEDAW, the *PfA* is not legally binding, nor is it fully comprehensive. For example, in the area of poverty, no commitment is made to reducing the feminization of poverty. However, the *PfA* is a major document and resource for advocates of sex equality. Notably, the process is built around particular targets and indicators against which progress may be measured.

In 2000, a meeting was held in New York to assess progress and revisit the *PfA*. Preparation for this meeting included reports by participating countries on their progress toward achieving the goals of the *Platform*, and meetings in participating countries of NGOs and between government and NGOs to discuss goals and demands. The New York meeting was known as Beijing+5, a reference to the five years that had passed since the 1995 World Congress.

Representing Parliamentarians for Global Action, Shazia Rafia gave an account of the New York meeting.[2] Many delegates at Wilton Park had also attended the New York meeting or been involved in preparing for it in some way. The report and ensuing discussion offered a mixed picture. The New York meeting was expected to be difficult. The 1999 International Conference on Population and Development (Cairo plus Five) saw fierce contestation of the targets and population policies long since agreed. In particular opponents of abortion policy and birth control attempted to gain control of UN population policy. However, according to Shazia Rafia, the 1999 experience mobilized women to come out in full force for Beijing+5. The numbers who wished to be official or NGO delegates overwhelmed the UN officers organizing the meeting. UN security attempted to control numbers by restricting passes and refusing entry.

The New York meeting was able to gain a good overview of progress on the *PfA*; 128 governments filed country reports. The conference recognized that the goals and commitments made in the *PfA* had not been fully implemented and achieved. The conference agreed on the need for further action and initiatives at local, national, regional and international levels. The objectives of the *Platform* were reaffirmed as the empowerment of all women regardless of reservations. Women's rights were reaffirmed as human rights, and the duty of states to promote and protect human rights was emphatically restated. In this context the New York meeting assessed progress in ten main areas of activity and identified new challenges.

Women and Poverty

It was recognized that many governments, in co-operation with NGOs, are making efforts to integrate a gender perspective into their eradication of poverty programmes. However, overall, the poverty gender gap is widening, as the experience of poverty is increasingly feminized.

Education and Training of Women

The importance of education to the achievement of sex equality was recognized. The meeting called on governments to encourage women to pursue all fields of study, especially the sciences, technological subjects and economics. Progress toward equality of education continues to be inhibited by lack of financial resources and insufficient political will.

Women and Health

Governments have begun to focus more on health programmes that cover aspects of women's health throughout the lifecycle. Such change has led to increased life expectancy for women. However, many obstacles continue, including endemic, infectious and communicable diseases, particularly HIV/AIDS. Other problems were insufficient services for adolescent girls and insufficient development of male contraceptive programmes. Better preventive health programmes are needed, including cancer prevention, osteoporosis prevention, prevention of tobacco use and the need to reduce recourse to abortion, which is a leading cause of maternal morbidity.

Violence Against Women

Violence against women is considered to be an issue of human rights. Governments have a duty to exercise due diligence to prevent, investigate and punish acts of violence. Many governments work actively in this area through mechanisms such as intergovernmental (inter-agency) committees. Policy on violence against women benefits from close co-operation between governments and NGOs. The obstacles to progress include an inadequate understanding of the root causes of violence against women and girls, and the lack of comprehensive programmes to deal with perpetrators. The spread of the use of information technology to assist trafficking in women and children was identified as a new area for policy.

Women and Armed Conflict

Armed conflict has a destructive effect on women. A gender-sensitive approach should be applied to the application of international law. The recognition of crimes against women by international criminal tribunals and the proposed international criminal court was acknowledged, as were those countries that have accepted sex discrimination at home as a basis for refugee status. However, many obstacles remain, including the failure by the UN itself to appoint women to decision-making positions in sufficient numbers, and especially as special envoys and representatives of the Secretary General. A further problem is that of internally displaced people who do not fit into UN definitions of refugees and are therefore not subject to UN agreements. So many armed conflicts are now internal that definitions must be changed to include those who are internally displaced as refugees. Finally military spending exhausted money and resources that were better spent on social development programmes.

Women in Power and Decision-making

The conference acknowledged the increase in absolute numbers of women in decision-making and cited the adoption of affirmative action plans to bring about change. However gaps between *de jure* and *de facto* policy continue.

Institutional Mechanisms for the Advancement of Women

Progress on women's rights through strategies of gender mainstreaming was cited by the conference, as was the ratification of CEDAW by 165 countries. However the goal of universal ratification has not been achieved.

Women and the Media

The conference bypassed the conventional media as barely worth trying to change. It focused instead upon the need to develop access to the Internet infrastructure, which is free of editorial and proprietary controls and therefore has the potential to be developed by its users.

Women and the Environment

Few government programmes have incorporated gender perspectives on the environment.

The Girl Child

The conference recognized that increasing legislation is in place against female genital mutilation. Governments have also made progress levying heavier penalties for the exploitation of the girl child. However the sexual abuse and exploitation of girls continues to increase.

New challenges

In the course of its discussion the conference identified a number of new challenges. These include:

- globalization and the resulting increase in the feminization of poverty
- trends toward increased privatization and the resulting loss of government funded childcare and other services and supports for employed women in countries in transition
- the absence of women from e-commerce
- the increasing migration of women and girls, including internal, regional and international migration
- the needs of older women, particularly older single women
- the impact of HIV/AIDS on both victims and caregivers.

In summary, governments and NGOs at the Beijing+5 meeting made a serious effort to assess progress and deal with obstacles and challenges. The conference was a site of continuous bargaining because so many of the issues that were discussed were contentious.

Discussion

The report from New York raised the issue of what the UN conferences on women have achieved. Achievement was understood in two distinct ways: first, the achievements of governments signed up to CEDAW, and second, the achievements of the conferences themselves. It was noted that governments have proved adept at avoiding the economic elements of the establishment or protection of women's rights.

On the one hand there is a danger that the process may be symbolic, mainly a paper-pushing exercise. However symbolic action often portends substantive action. The New York meeting required governments and NGOs to report on the *Platform for Action*, hence it has enhanced the legitimacy of the process. People gather to prepare the documents and negotiate their contents. Others read and report about the conference. Many read the documents. Yet, although they legitimize policies on women's rights in domestic politics, international meetings are very expensive and the budget for action on women is very limited. Are large expensive meetings the best use of resources? Does the process on which they are focused offer substantial improvements in the status of women? Such questions are of increasing concern both to participants and to observers of the Beijing process.

Notes

1 Based on the presentation by Shazia Rafia, Secretary General, and Parliamentarians for Global Action.

2 Parliamentarians for Global Action is an association of 13 000 members from ninety-nine parliaments.

7 Gender mainstreaming[1]

Since the early 1990s gender mainstreaming has been regarded as the most effective strategy for effecting equality between the sexes. In its ideal form it is applied to all areas of policy and decision-making. It is defined in the Beijing *Platform for Action* as the process whereby governments and other actors promote an active and visible policy of mainstreaming a gender perspective into all policies and programmes so that, before decisions are taken, an analysis is made of the effects on both women and men. Its purpose is to ensure that policies do not disadvantage women.

Gender mainstreaming is an equality strategy that covers policies, laws and their implementation across the whole range of government activities. Such policy is made with an explicit consideration of its differential impacts on women and men and with the intention of ensuring equality of opportunity and equity of outcome. In practical terms a commitment to gender mainstreaming has at least four implications.

1. Laws must be reviewed for discriminatory or constraining provisions.
2. Laws must be analysed to identify vague aspects that might produce interpretations that would work to the disadvantage of women (or others).
3. Laws must be supplemented to address disadvantage and discrimination.
4. Laws should be developed in a framework of procedures that require all legislation to be gender-sensitive.

Real gender mainstreaming is very difficult, featuring many of the problems that were experienced in previous generations of sex equality policy. It requires political will and high-level support. Commitment to its principles needs to be organization wide. It presupposes that there are growing numbers of women in decision-making positions who work (with men) to implement it. Moreover, the policy depends upon the existence of individuals who have specialist skills, tools and methods of equality including sex-disaggregated data and gender-sensitive indicators of progress to facilitate monitoring of policy effects.

How does gender mainstreaming work in practice? The practice of gender mainstreaming follows the same general principles but is necessarily adapted to the culture and goals of the organization in which it is being implemented. The necessity to adapt is illustrated by two examples of the implementation of gender mainstreaming in development politics.

The first example is that of gender mainstreaming in OECD development co-operation. In 1995, following the production of the Beijing *Platform for Action*, the Development Assistance Committee (DAC) adopted a high-level statement: *Gender Equality: Moving Toward Sustainable Development*. In this statement the DAC committed to gender equality and to gender mainstreaming as a strategy to improve development outcomes, tackle gender disparities and uphold respect for women's human rights. The policy was reviewed after five years as part of the preparation for Beijing+5.

The review identified areas of progress and areas of continuing challenge for the DAC. Progress had been made on the integration of gender sensitivity into the work on human rights, good governance, conflict resolution, participatory development and the reduction of poverty. Policy dialogue had become more gender-sensitive and more inclusive. Good work had been done in supporting and building the capacity of women's organizations.

However many challenges remained. The review concluded that gender mainstreaming could be made more effective if it had stronger high-level management support, better resourcing, more sharing of good practice, more specialist expertise, better data and better measures of progress. The overall verdict was that good progress had been made, but more could have been achieved.

The second example is that of mainstreaming in a Department for International Development (DFID) country programme. In this case study work began with a gender audit that produced a template against which progress could be measured. The gender audit is a tool that policy makers can use to identify gender dimensions of policy and government decision-making. It can take many forms and it should be part of the toolkit of gender mainstreaming policy.

One interesting feature of the gender audits of country programmes is that they reveal long-standing and widely known problems and obstacles encountered in the implementation of experiences of equality policy. This does not mean that no progress has been made; rather it suggests that there are recurring themes in the experiences of implementing equality policy. These include the continuing need to get support throughout organizations and to insist that other priorities are not allowed to override the goal of gender equality.

The DFID found that gender mainstreaming is most effectively implemented:

- where management support at all levels is strong
- where systems, procedures and activities promote gender equality
- where staff has gender expertise
- where resources are adequate
- where tools and methods are available to treat 'harder cases'
- where partner governments and agencies share a commitment to gender equality
- where practical information and support is readily available
- where a mandate exists.

Discussion

The gender mainstreaming strategy was discussed in some detail. Delegates wanted more information on its practicalities. Many had experience of attempting to implement gender mainstreaming in different contexts, and offered a number of observations on the problems of implementation and how to overcome them. Three main problems were discussed: resources including money and aid, ethnic diversity and the problems of implementation in multicultural societies, and the effects of globalization.

Practicalities

Delegates most wanted to know how to do gender mainstreaming. The opening questioner asked why the OECD decided to gender mainstream, how management interest and support was obtained and what part agencies such as the DAC and government departments such as the DFID could play in facilitating good gender mainstreaming policy. Follow-up questions were about how to implement the policy into particular areas. A number of examples were described. In the case of South African child welfare it was found that the gender assumptions underlying the original design of child benefit policy resulted in misdirecting the benefit. Originally the makers of benefit policy assumed that the primary carers of children were women, and that for any particular child the carer would be his or her mother. In fact often women other than the mother looked after children, hence many benefits were not finding their object, the child. The solution was to direct benefit toward the child and his or her carer rather than the mother.

Gender mainstreaming requires an imaginative rethinking of policy problems at the beginning of the policy process. This in turn requires good communications between policy makers and groups of women. In Italy for example, Milan and some other cities audited their services and hours to determine whether they were convenient for both women and men. In India, every ministry has a special unit that examines programmes of the ministry for gender effect, a process overseen by a separate Ministry for Women. This process connects to a Parliamentary Committee on Women's Rights, and aims to weed out contradictions and unfair gender effects. The example of the UK Cabinet Office Women's Unit was offered as a mechanism to implement gender mainstreaming in government. The unit is intended to open up Whitehall to gender concerns. It was suggested that such a unit might be better situated in the Treasury because the Treasury has oversight of all government spending.

In Northern Europe, women's organizations have been very effective in identifying and changing practices that are inhospitable to women. In Weimar, a strong women's group has made the town more women-friendly, with well lit streets and car parks, thereby removing the protection of darkness from would be rapists. In the Nordic states, gender impact assessment of legislation was first implemented some years ago, and is continually being adjusted and reworked to take account of experience

Problems

The design and implementation of gender mainstreaming policy requires attention to resources, ethnic diversity and the impact of globalization.

Resources

A repeated theme of the discussion was the need for sufficient resources for effective gender mainstreaming. Resources included skills and expertise and money – all difficult to obtain.

Money could be made available from domestic budgets or from aid budgets of various kinds. Many delegates felt that international aid agencies should demand gender equity policies before aid was distributed. But, such a policy may not have the desired effects. Phil Evans indicated that the DFID was reluctant to adopt such a blanket principle because a lot of poor countries have bad governments and the department was reluctant to punish their populations. Instead, its strategy was to assess their own performance, to use scales to judge DFID performance, which, it was thought, would have long-term beneficial effects in aid taking countries.

The point was also made that gender mainstreaming is expensive and many poor countries cannot afford to prioritize it. Questions were raised about how to gender mainstream hospitals and schools. Delegates reported significant gender insensitivities in the aid programmes of international organizations. The European Union came in for sharp criticism over the gender blindness of its external relations directorates. Repeated suggestions were made that debt rescheduling, donations and aid should be tied to the status of women in the society and the economy of the recipient country. Under such a regime a country seeking funds would be required to show effective and appropriate gender mainstreaming strategies. Evidence should be at least partly financial: national budgets would be expected to contain detailed provision for gender mainstreaming under every functional heading.

Ethnic Diversity

It should not be assumed that gender mainstreaming would take place in a homogenous society. Strategies were needed to take account of ethnic differences and the competing priorities that ethnic differences generated. However gender difference is common to all ethnic groups and while ethnic difference must be taken into account, the principles of listening to women, ensuring their representation and monitoring their social, economic and political status continue to be the hallmarks of gender-sensitive policy.

Globalization

The effects of globalization on women are part of the effects of globalization on the poor. The analysis of its impact suggests mixed patterns. Change in traditional patterns of production has created women entrepreneurs working in co-operatives from their homes. The transfer of production (for example, textiles) from one part of the world to another benefits some groups of women and displaces others. Globalization is an omnibus concept and a complex process that varies in its effects on gender relations.

The discussion showed that there was considerable interest in sharing experiences of gender mainstreaming so that good practice could be transferred among countries and policy areas. Funding was perceived to be a widespread problem and gender auditing, especially of budgets, a promising corrective. Overall effective gender policy was thought to depend upon asking the right questions and working closely with women's organizations.

Note

1 Based on the presentation by Dr Phil Evans, Senior Adviser and Deputy Head of Social Development, Department for International Development, London.

8 Affirmative action: help or hindrance[1]

Is affirmative action a legitimate strategy for addressing inequalities between groups? How might affirmative action be used in conjunction with other strategies?

Affirmative action can be a powerful tool for adjusting inequalities. However it is controversial, and it often generates or sustains backlash against equality policies. To discuss it properly it is necessary to be clear about its definition. Affirmative action emerged out of the US civil rights movements of the 1960s and 1970s. It calls for minorities, women and other disadvantaged groups to be given special consideration in employment, education and contracting decisions. Institutions with affirmative action policies generally set goals and timetables for increased diversity using recruitment preferences and targets as the means of reaching their goals. In its modern form affirmative action can call for an admissions officer, faced with two similarly qualified applicants, to choose the member of the minority group. Or a manager might in that circumstance hire a qualified woman in preference to a similarly qualified man. In this definition affirmative action decisions are not based on quotas (understood as compulsory targets), nor do they give any preference to unqualified candidates. However, they should alert us to imbalances in our qualification criteria so that we reassess qualifications and how we understand merit in a gender-sensitive manner. In other words affirmative action is not reverse discrimination. Moreover, affirmative action is a temporary and partial remedy for past and continuing discrimination against historically marginalized and disenfranchised groups. It is probably also flawed. In its best manifestations affirmative action affords greater equality of opportunity in a social context marked by substantial inequalities and structural forces that impede fair assessment of the qualifications of members of disadvantaged groups.

Controversial as it is, affirmative action is the subject of increasing debate and tension in societies that are attempting to address gender and other inequalities. Unfortunately the debate has become cloaked in a rhetoric that pits equality of opportunity against equality of results. The debate has progressively become more emotional than intellectual and as a result, has confused rather than illuminated the issue. In many cases participants in the debate have become fixated on the ethical and moral dimensions raised, and consequently neglected the scrutiny of the system that created the need for them.

Yet inequalities continue. In the case of women, only eight countries have achieved (Sweden, Denmark, Finland and Norway) or come near to achieving (Iceland, Netherlands, Germany and South Africa) sex equality in secondary education, political representation and share of employment; elsewhere, in both developing and developed countries, there is a long way to go.[2]

The Debate on Affirmative Action: Examples and Arguments

Opposition to affirmative action is bitter and widespread. Opponents argue that the battle to guarantee equal rights for all citizens has been fought, both nationally and internationally, and won – and that favouring one group over another goes against the grain of rights for all. In the United Kingdom affirmative action is unlawful, and is considered contrary to the legislative provisions of the Sex Discrimination and Equal Pay Acts. In spite of legislation requiring equal pay for work of equal value, women working full time in 1999 were less well paid than men were by a factor of about 20 per cent (women's full time average hourly earnings were 81 per cent of men's). In other words the evidence suggests that current equality policy is insufficient and something more is needed to level the playing field.

Critics of affirmative action also argue that such policies stigmatize and call into question the credentials of qualified women and minorities. This doubt undermines their effectiveness. Co-workers may be uncooperative and the individual will always doubt that he or she should be there. In response to this contention it is argued that affirmative action can give minorities the opportunities to defy the stereotypes and stigmas cast upon them by others. Arguably the failure to use affirmative action will continue the exclusion of women and minorities and further ingrain the stereotypes and stigmas that inhibit their progress and reduce their self-esteem.

Affirmative Action in Political Representation

Political representation, defined as presence in elected or appointed decision-making bodies, is an important indicator of progress toward sex equality in a society. Many countries have adopted affirmative action strategies to enhance women's political representation. In 1995, the Fifth Meeting of Commonwealth Ministers Responsible for Women's Affairs expressed support for affirmative action to increase women's participation to at least 30 per cent of the relevant fora. This decision was taken against a background of action in the different countries. In the Commonwealth two broad types of affirmative action have been adopted:

- Constitutional or legally defined quotas, for example in India, Tanzania and Uganda, up to one-third of local government seats are reserved for women.
- Action by political parties including quotas and targets of women candidates and officials. Such action has been taken in South Africa, Mozambique, Canada, Australia and the United Kingdom, where major parties have made significant strides in increasing the number of women on their candidates' lists.

Such measures have had significant effects (see Table 8.1). Quotas and targets are a very useful means of enhancing women's representation. These devices should be understood as being part of a process in which other aspects of inequality are being targeted and in which representation increases in women's presence in one part of the system often lead to increases in another. The Commonwealth Ministers responsible for Women's Affairs have stressed the importance of

Table 8.1. Women's representation in political decision-making in the Commonwealth: Ranking of top ten countries in 1999/2000

	National Executive/Cabinet (1999)	%	*National Parliament (2000)*	%	*Local government (1999)*	%
1	The Gambia	30.8	South Africa	30.3	Seychelles	54.0
2	South Africa	29.6	New Zealand	29.3	Uganda	40.8
3	Grenada	26.7	Mozambique	28.0	India	33.5
4	Sierra Leone	26.4	Australia	25.0	Canada	30.0
5	Seychelles	25.0	Seychelles	23.5	New Zealand	29.0
6	Canada	24.0	Canada	22.2	St. Lucia	29.0
7	United Kingdom	22.0	Trinidad & Tobago	20.9	United Kingdom	27.0
8	Mozambique	19.6	Bahamas	19.6	Australia	24.0
9	Botswana	19.0	Belize	18.4	Trinidad & Tobago	20.4
10	Uganda	18.6	Uganda	18.3	St. Vincent & the Grenadines	20.0

ensuring that positive and affirmative action to get more women into positions of decision-making was accompanied by training, mentoring and other forms of support so that once elected or appointed, women are able to play the political game.

Affirmative Action in the Workplace: Reconciling Work and Family

It is difficult to exaggerate the changes in the nature and composition of the paid workforce during the past fifty years. Such changes are part of a wider process in which family structures have also changed and patterns of employment and family life need to be adjusted to fit each other. In the United States for example, many employers have failed to recognize that in most families both spouses work. This is reflected in wage differentials and in attitudes toward the position of women workers. There continues to be a view that women are not in the workforce on equal terms to men because they do not want to be, they prefer to prioritize their traditional roles. Yet the real position is much more complicated.

Enlightened employers understand that the world is changing and that responding to such changes is in their interests. Most couples are happy with two-career lifestyles. Women who return to work after childbearing normally do so because they want to, not because they have to. However, these working women face considerable conflicts of role overload – wife, mother, and career professional. Spouses look not only to each other, but also to employers when they seek to balance work and home life.

To meet these expectations employers need to go beyond affirmative action and establish family-friendly employment policies. US research has shown that such policies are extremely beneficial to the companies that adopt them, reducing staff turnover and increasing employee motivation and loyalty.

What are family-friendly employment policies? The best policies include six main elements:

- Flexibility over hours and conditions: options include flexitime, work sharing, and telecommuting.
- Listen to employees: family-friendly companies survey their employees about work and life topics in order to develop employee driven work/life initiatives. Examples include lactation rooms, phase-back for new mothers, childcare subsidies, before and after school and summertime care and paternity leave.
- Communicate policies: family-friendly policies are well publicized within the company and employees are encouraged to use them. The policies are sold to employees and continuing efforts are made to avoid stigmas from the use of 'mommy-track' career options.
- Career development: family-friendly companies take an active interest in optimizing the potential for female staff. They have programmes of mentoring, on-site training and study leave. Policies are monitored and adjusted. In some companies manager pay is tied to the advancement of female staff.
- Compensation: companies offer high pay, savings options, pensions, health insurance and stock purchase plans.
- Zero tolerance of sexual harassment.

The companies themselves benefit. As the sophistication of their work/life policies increases, so do bottom line benefits. The good work environment created for women and men produces real returns. For example, the comprehensive resource and referral programme at Prudential saved the company US$7 million in reduced absenteeism and staff turnover. The giant company CIGNA reported that its lactation programme reduced absenteeism by new mothers by 27 per cent. Benjamin Group's on-site childcare and twenty-four week maternity leave, combined with a company culture that values women, keeps turnover low. Each time Benjamin fills a post without using a headhunter the company saves US$20 000. Such measures are now also part of political life. For example, the British Prime Minister Tony Blair took time off to be with his wife and new son born while he was in office, although he resisted his wife's public call to take full paternity leave.

Men

Family-friendly employment policies benefit both women and men. However it is clear that men experience considerable resistance when they reject single-minded careerism and seek to balance work and family life. Suzanne Braun Levine has written about these problems in her book *Father Courage: What Happens When Men Put Family First?* Her conclusion is that measures are needed to support this growing group of men.

In conclusion, affirmative action is a necessary but not sufficient measure in equal opportunity policies. However, on its own it cannot deliver equality of outcome. Equality of outcome requires additional measures. In particular, gender mainstreaming and the Commonwealth Secretariat's Gender Management System offer effective means of enhancing equality (see chapters 20 and 21).

Discussion

The successful use of affirmative action strategies involves six main issues: the practicalities, legislation, education, the role of NGOs, the necessity of economic independence for women and the backlash.

Practicalities

There is no popularly accepted common definition of affirmative action. Some wondered if it was the same as positive action, others equated it with reverse discrimination. It is often felt that no matter how affirmative action or its cognates are defined, some kind of special treatment was essential to produce a level playing field between women and men. Setting targets must be complemented with practical strategies including internal reorganization and the establishment or upgrading of equality machinery in firms, agencies and political parties. Generally public agencies are more hospitable to affirmative action than private firms. National action plans on gender should be accompanied by gendered national action plans on other issues and policy areas; this is the essence of gender mainstreaming. Carrot and stick approaches are very important to successful legislation. Many argue that in a good gender mainstreaming system a separate women's ministry is less important that effective equality officers at departmental level. However, co-ordination is essential to good policy. Therefore an effective system of equality officers is required. A responsible minister at senior government level is often the most appropriate institutional mechanism for the co-ordination of equality policy.

It is important to treat affirmative action as a temporary measure and to regard it as a process. At first it is a goal and must be lobbied for. Once established it needs to be monitored, adjusted and developed as thresholds are crossed and the perceptions of needs change. For example political parties have changed in order to win more women voters, creating a different environment in which different affirmative action strategies should be developed. Changing underlying political attitudes is a long process, one of the goals of affirmative action.

Legislation

Constitutional or legislative quotas are very strong measures. In India the Minster for Women was accused of being 'westernized' when she supported a one-third quota of women in local office. The quotas have brought over 1 million women into elected office and in the minister's own state 45 per cent of elected local officials are women. One effect of this gender change in local office is that women have adopted grass roots based priorities in their policy preferences, demanding drinking water, better health and better education. The Indian women's advocates used the expertise of development scholars (from Sussex University) to devise their affirmative action programmes. Indian equality policies include internal quotas in political parties, a provision that is also a feature of many Commonwealth and European democracies.

Education

Issues of education were raised by delegates who were exercised by the failure of boys at school, a phenomenon that many considered to be a part of the backlash against the achievements of women. However if 70 per cent of university students in some countries are women and boys are performing badly, why are not women getting the best jobs? The importance of education in changing attitudes to gender was reaffirmed.

Role of NGOs

There is a considerable part to be played by NGOs in publicizing gender mainstreaming approaches and in combating the opposition to women's equality. NGOs can also maintain registers of qualified women, and combat in practical terms the argument that there are not enough qualified women. In Canada strong lobbying women's associations have campaigned effectively to increase women's presence in government.

Necessity of Economic Independence for Women

Affirmative action policies should be located in a context in which women are able to act independently and are therefore in a position to take up and make use of political opportunities. However, processes of globalization whereby women have been increasingly excluded from the processes and benefits of economic restructuring may have hindered the effects of affirmative action policies. On the other hand such processes have led to the establishment of home-based small enterprises led by women who are finding a new economic base.

Backlash

Backlash appears to take many forms. The widespread failure of boys at school is sometimes attributed to the effects of progress toward women's equality. Trivialization of the work of women is another form of backlash as is not taking women's representation seriously. Many delegates cited the lack of legitimacy of 'quota women' as a backlash effect.

Conclusions

The implementation of affirmative action puts into sharp relief the complexity of the processes of bringing about equality between the sexes. Stereotypes, social conditions and attitudes and measurable inequalities in pay, conditions and representation all contribute to a complex and pressing problem.

Notes

1 Based on a presentation by Nancy Spence, Director, Gender and Youth Affairs Division, Commonwealth Secretariat.

2 United Nations, *The World's Women 2000: Trends and Statistics.*

9 Education and sex equality[1]

Education is properly considered to be a central component of sex equality policy throughout the Commonwealth and elsewhere. Various policies have been developed to ensure that girls have the same opportunities as boys and to ensure the access of adult women to education programmes. Three issues recur in discussions of education policy and sex equality:

1. Education policy should be designed in ways that ensure it is delivered to girls and women.
2. The problem of boys and men needs to be addressed. Where women are getting access to education, it sometimes creates new problems, possibly because of male perceptions of displacement.
3. The impact of education on women's empowerment should be considered. There is considerable evidence that the educational achievements of women do not translate into access to political power.

Each of these issues plays out in different ways in different countries, but the general trends are strikingly similar.

Deficits in educational provision for girls and women are a widely recognized problem. The Platform for Action adopted by the Fourth World Conference on Women in Beijing identified the need to ensure women's full and equal access to education and training as one of twelve critical areas requiring urgent attention by governments and the international community. Two contrasting examples illustrate both the importance of educational policy and the early effects of equalizing educational provision: India and the Bahamas.

India

India has devised a substantial programme of education for equality. According to Dr Alva, provision includes a range of policies designed to get girls into education and keep them there. Policy makers and educators recognize that women are 50 per cent of the world's human resource and its largest group of marginalized citizens. The marginalization of women has been sanctified by religion, continued by custom, dogged by illiteracy, economic dependence, and lack of self-esteem – problems Alva considers to be universal. Critical areas include the problem of high levels of illiteracy among adult women, the low numbers of girls in technical and vocational education and their absence from science and engineering subjects. About 75 per cent of women aged 25 and above cannot read and write in much of Asia and Africa. In southern Asia only 40 girls per 100 boys are enrolled at secondary school, only 9 per cent in Afghanistan, and 17 per cent in Pakistan. In India 72 per cent of men are literate but only 50 per cent of women. Education policy in India has had to overcome cultural resistances of various kinds. For example child marriages and female infanticide are still practised.

Adopted in 1987, the law on education for equality is a relatively recent phenomenon. The law states that education will be used as an agent of basic change in the status of women. In order to neutralize the accumulated distortions of the past, there will be an 'edge in favour of women'. This will be an act of faith and social engineering. The removal of women's illiteracy and of the obstacles inhibiting their access to and retention in elementary education will receive overriding priority, through provision of special support services, setting times and targets and reflective monitoring.

Among the measures taken to implement the Indian policy is the provision of special incentives to get girls into schools, including provision by the state of books, midday meals and uniforms. Incentives have been established for sending and keeping girls in school; in some states monthly allowances are paid to parents who keep girls in schools. Day care centres are attached to primary schools so that schoolgirls can bring the younger siblings for whom they have caring responsibilities. Textbooks are examined for gender bias and the curriculum is being revised to remove bias. In rural areas schools run double shifts, one for boys and one for girls, in order to get past taboos about coeducation. Women teachers are employed because girls cannot be sent to male teachers. The women teachers are role models. To offset the pattern whereby women teachers are overwhelmingly concentrated in primary schools, more women are being employed at secondary and tertiary level. Co-education is being introduced wherever possible at the pre-school and primary level to ensure gender-sensitization and an equal start in life. Vocational and skills training programmes are being targeted at girls, particularly in male dominated professions. Hostel facilities are offered to girls from remote and rural areas wishing to continue their education. Distance learning, condensed courses and adult education complete the programme. Women's studies courses have been set up in the universities. Gender-sensitization programmes are used in the training of teachers and education planners.

The wider effects of differences in educational access for boys and girls are keenly felt in India. The problem of adult illiteracy is enormous, and characterized by a gender gap whereby women are more likely than men to be illiterate, a problem that impedes the state's ability to inform women about opportunities. However, there are many encouraging signs that new policies are having an effect. For example, computer training has become popular with girls because it can be home based. Girls do better than boys in examinations; more women than men vote.

In India the challenge is to change the cultural mindset. Regular campaigns are conducted to persuade parents to allow girls to take up opportunities. Such campaigns need to be combined with campaigns against practices such as the dowry system. Political education is increasing and women's studies centres have been established all over the country. NGOs, local government and educational institutions have launched campaigns aimed at removing obstacles to the achievements of women and girls. These include campaigns on literacy, legal, economic and political rights, health and population control, childcare, nutrition and hygiene, violence in the family, alcohol abuse and HIV. Programmes of training are offered to improve self-esteem and self-confidence, in leadership development, organizing and networking and political participation.

The Bahamas

A contrasting example is that of the Bahamas where women were successful, but male achievement became an acute problem. Dr Bernard Nottage has described the way Bahamian education policy has related to developments in democratic politics. The Bahamas are a 27-year-old nation with 281 years of experience of parliamentary democracy. However, that democracy was won through struggle and it is frequently tested. In terms of equality, from 1953, when the first political party was formed, one of its goals was to establish political equality. Originally equality was understood in terms of voting and government – the objective was to establish majority rule. Inequalities were perceived as racially based, and black Bahamians came to understand that a franchise based on property was a means to keep the minority white population in power. Education was regarded as a crucial means to establish political equality. Women were not originally included and were not enfranchised until 1962. Even then they were not given real opportunities to enter Parliament and did not stand for 'safe seats' until the 1980s.

However, women excelled at education, which has proved to a great equalizer for women and in some respects a marginalizer of men. Between 1968 and 1978 Bahamian education was massively expanded. Secondary education was made available on all of the islands. In 1975, the College of the Bahamas was established so that more Bahamian students could pursue higher education. Previously tertiary education was available only abroad. Women in large numbers and men in fewer numbers took advantage of the expansion. Education opened opportunities for many new careers for both sexes. Men were no longer confined to careers in the civil service and women no longer restricted to a life at home. Many women stayed in the education system as teachers; today women are 79 per cent of the teaching profession. Men pursued the more lucrative careers of law, medicine, banking, insurance and accounting. They took advantage of an expanding economy and entered tourism and related industries. Others found careers in expanding building and construction trades. The economy flourished. Tourism and banking, the principal industries, led an economic shift that gave the Bahamas the third highest standard of living in the Western hemisphere. In the mid-1990s UNESCO confirmed GDP at US$11 790. This prosperity led to migration from neighbouring countries, especially Haiti, Jamaica and the Turks and Caicos Islands.

Social change accompanied economic change, and effects were particularly felt in changing family structures. In 1965 70 per cent of live births were to married women, but by 2000 75 per cent of live births were to single women. Forty per cent of homes are single headed, and of these 60 per cent are led by women. Materialism is on the increase and traditional morality in decline. The gap between rich and poor has widened: 3 per cent of Bahamians control 80 per cent of the nations' wealth. Crime, particularly violent crime, has escalated. The archipelago has proved a useful transhipment area for drugs bound for the United States, creating a number of related problems. The minority merchant class continues to be as powerful as it was before majority rule.

Within large-scale social change the problem of the marginalization of boys in education began to emerge. More women than men are studying in universities abroad, and more women have been awarded academic scholarships. Men are in the minority in the College of the Bahamas, where 800 of the 3000 students are men. This pattern is repeated throughout the English-speaking Caribbean, and is likely to continue. Primary school teachers report more boys than girls in remedial classes. At secondary level in the 1999 BGCSE examinations, taken at the end of twelfth grade, women candidates obtained 60 per cent of A–C grades. Women teachers outnumber their male colleagues by three to one in the public school system; men are 40 per cent of school administrators. In short, education is a women's domain.

How can the various gender imbalances in education be corrected? The Bahamian Ministry of Education aims to provide everyone with the opportunities for education that will equip them for work and life in a democratic country. Education policy does not in its current form include a plan to redress gender imbalances, yet equality goals will not be met without gender-sensitive education policy.

Despite their absence from the education system men outnumber women in politics. The first woman Member of the Parliament was elected in 1982. In 1997, both major parties offered only six women candidates (out of forty). Women deputies are overloaded, and all have additional parliamentary responsibilities. The current Parliament has six women deputies, five of whom are in the governing party. Two are government ministers, one is the Speaker and one is the Chief Whip. The sixth is a backbencher. The woman member of the opposition party is deputy party leader and Opposition Whip. Men continue to lead the church and are the overwhelming majority in the legal profession, in law enforcement, the construction trade, auto mechanics, agriculture and fisheries. However, women are entering previously male-dominated professions in increasing numbers. The public services are beginning to attract many women. Thus eight of fourteen Permanent Secretaries are women, 52 per cent of computer programmers are women, and 35 per cent of lawyers and 24 per cent of doctors are women. The majority of interns at the main hospital are women. Women make up 95 per cent of nurses and 74 per cent of teachers.

Further evidence of the marginalization of Bahamian males is that the ratio of male to female prisoners is 33:1. Many more men than women appear daily before the courts. Some psychologists take the view that the increase in crime against women is a manifestation of the Bahamian male's struggle to retain power. Such ideas are probably too simplistic. Nevertheless the problem is there, and there is a need for education policy to deal with male underachievement. Two problems are especially pressing. First is the problem of absentee fathers and its impact on boys' self-esteem and the nature of the household. Second, boys and men apparently feel uncomfortable and threatened in schools and other parts of society by the preponderance of women. Education experts have made various policy suggestions:

1. Vigorously address the problem of basic literacy at primary school level and for older boys.
2. Make self-esteem development a core part of the curriculum.
3. Develop indigenous materials for students that offer positive male images and role models.
4. Customize the curriculum to the local economies.
5. Recruit more male teachers and upgrade the teaching profession so that salary and conditions are commensurate with professions that require similar qualifications.

6. Reintroduce all-male schools.
7. Train teachers, especially women teachers, to better meet the needs of male students.
8. Use technology in the classroom to excite boys about its uses and applications.
9. Involve more men in the life of the school.
10. Offer parenting classes beginning at junior high school levels.

Most such policies were originally devised to improve the status of women. Education then is potentially able to address different kinds of gender imbalances, offering not only training but also the opportunities to enhance self-esteem and remake cultural values.

Discussion

The problem of boys is fairly widespread, but its effects are less dramatic in some countries, at least so far. Policy makers must be careful when addressing this problem to avoid fuelling a backlash that will create barriers for women without improving matters for boys. Despite the emerging problem of male underachievement and male absence from family life, women are not equal in terms of pay, power or prestige. Educational success has not translated into political success. Is this a 'lag' effect that will disappear with time, or is something more pernicious going on? How can education alter the commitment of men to fatherhood and family life? How can change be effected when it is essential that girls prepare for a life that is economically independent? Such questions are insistent and difficult. The political experience of education for equality, central as it is, raises more problems than it offers solutions. The theme of education was raised in almost all the conference discussions; its potential to solve problems was repeatedly invoked. Yet when it came to hard cases, delegates were puzzled and uncertain.

Note

1 Based on the presentations by Dr Margaret Alva MP and Dr Bernard Nottage MP.

10 Equalizing access to care and services[1]

Access to health and education and protection from the effects of poverty are crucial to sex equality. Although women are major providers of care and services, they frequently have less access to them than do men. The problem that governments must address is that of how to equalize and at the same time improve services for women.

What strategies will best provide equitable access to health care and social services?' Three assumptions are implicit in this question:

- There is inequitable access.
- Problems of inequitable access should be solved.
- Improved access for women is desirable.

In communities all over the world women are denied access to health care and social services by reason of poverty, sex discrimination, lack of education, poor information and deeply ingrained social mores. The need to improve women's access to health care is one of the twelve points of the Beijing Platform for Action. The problem is widely recognized. Several approaches have been used to improve services for women, with varying success. Recognizing that their human capital is a valuable resource, some countries have sought to create universal access to care and social services for all citizens. Others have developed care and service modules that specifically target females, a term used to indicate that equity of access is a problem for women and girls of all ages.

For all societies the provision of services for women is a desirable and necessary thing, not only on equality grounds, but also because women are child bearers and child rearers. For the most part it is women who nurture families, transmit social values and care for and socialize members of society. When women are unable to perform the roles of giving birth and providing care, it harms society. In short, just access to care and services is a means of providing for both sexes. The healthy, well-informed woman raises a better family and contributes to a better society. This persuasive argument, of course, contains assumptions about women's roles that understandably provoke considerable disagreement. However, the central points, that access to health care and social services should be equitable and that the provision of equitable access will benefit society as a whole, are not controversial.

Care and Services

Elizabeth Thompson uses the term 'care and services' to mean the amalgam of services including health, education and social-welfare, and those other state or quasi-state services that cater to the individual and the family. How can such services contribute to equality between the sexes? How can their provision be made equitable? The core problem is fundamental inequality between the sexes, a phenomenon that needs to be broken down into its constituent parts if it is to be understood and treated. In the case of care and services there are three main sex-differentiated barriers to equitable access: poverty, cultural attitudes and lack of information (ignorance).

Poverty

Women are the overwhelming majority of the world's poor; hence the treatment of poverty needs always to be gender-sensitive. Thompson believes that every member of society has a right to health care, education and social services. An individual's capacity to enjoy life, to function effectively and to contribute to national life and development depends on his or her health and state of mind. State of mind here means intellectual training, self-esteem and social standing. In societies where poverty is endemic the development of both the individual and the society alike are distorted. There is an almost symbiotic relationship between poverty and poor health; each is a cause and effect of the other. This self-reinforcing and sustaining cycle must be broken in order to liberate the individual and the society from its grip.

Available international data indicate that developing countries have two main types of health profile. Either they mirror developed countries with chronic non-communicable diseases as the major causes of death or disability, or their profile is of the diseases that stem from under-nutrition and under-supply of remedies. The challenge for developing countries is to find the resources to remedy their particular problem. One way to do that is to define a package of services necessary for the individual and then to budget for the provision of the services in that package. Far too often developing countries attempt to provide services using technology that is rapidly changing and unaffordable. Hence service delivery is compromised.

To provide proper services and make them available to the widest number of people, policy decisions must be made about what level of care and services, primary, secondary and tertiary, will be delivered to women in particular. Such inclusion of gender considerations in national budgeting processes is an equality strategy that has been enthusiastically taken up by women's advocacy organizations and equality professionals worldwide.

Some societies have yet to determine whether women are allowed to work, and if so allowed, whether they will get the same pay for doing the same job as their male counterparts. Available statistics suggest that in many countries there are fewer women in the labour force than men, that women are frequently confined to menial jobs, and that women's work is inequitably valued in comparison with men's work. In addition, unemployment more often affects women than men (except in the United Kingdom in the 1990s). All these factors combine to feminize poverty. Where access to care and services is not free, then women are less able to secure them.

Cultural Attitudes

While family care has traditionally been organized by women – as mothers, sisters and grandmothers – leadership has been left to men. The division of labour denies women power and autonomy.

It is underpinned by ingrained attitudinal and cultural biases that restrict women's access to care and services. Such barriers will be broken down only when it is agreed that women have value. Before equality can be developed it must be recognized that women have a valid contribution to make to their societies that goes beyond their reproductive and nurturing roles. The relationship between the sexes need not be adversarial. Many women do not want to usurp the roles of men; they want a justice and equality based upon a fair evaluation of their contribution.

The means of changing damaging cultural attitudes is through education at the community level. Women frequently have to be persuaded that they need access to care and services, to power and so on. Mechanisms must be developed to train leaders in the community in new values and attitudes, and then to let those leaders educate groups of women in homes, churches, at the river, the pipe, anywhere that women gather. Such structures are appropriate to the communities of women. Far too frequently policy makers build formal institutions and centres and then bring women to those centres. Greater success will be achieved if the message is taken to the community, using the vernacular and recognizing the local patterns of activity.

The organization of public education campaigns that target women can sometimes be linked to children's events. For example, women gather when mothers bring children into medical facilities for mass immunization campaigns. This is an opportunity to talk with them, to do their Pap smears or to give them the information they need. Joint educational classes for mothers and children where both learn to read or learn other skills together and help one another are also possible ways forward.

Lack of Information

Ignorance helps to sustain biases in cultural attitudes. Misinformation sanctioned by elders and strengthened by repetition and time is a problem in many societies. Good information campaigns to ensure myths are not perpetrated are critical. The use of the media, traditional teachers and of community leaders is central to reaching the target audience. A false belief, long and strongly held, is often difficult to dislodge. Traditional beliefs often serve to keep people in poverty and sometimes lead women to refuse care and services. Change at this level typically takes a very long time.

Sometimes, however, ignorance is not ignorance of the truth but lack of good information about available services and about how to get the services, compounded by timidity in claiming them. Information in such communities needs to be offered sensitively, using community leaders and non-electronic methods to convey the message.

The Potential of the Law

Legislation can be used to improve women's access to care and services and to accelerate social changes. In Barbados five measures have been especially significant:

- The Family Law Act established women's right to property and provided for the valuation of housework.
- The Status of Children Reform Act removed bastardy and gave succession rights to children of unmarried parents.
- The Amendment to the Health Services Act compelled people to hook up to the sewage system.
- The Education Act requires that all children be sent to school.
- The Ministry for Transformation was established with a gender equality brief.

Conclusion

In summary, women's access to health care and social services can be improved. Creative policy decisions are necessary to bring about attitudinal change by diminishing social and cultural prejudices. In addition the eradication or general reduction of poverty will be of particular benefit to women. Public education campaigns must be built on community customs, making use of local leaders. Such principles will generate more effective policy.

Discussion

The construction of a policy model that is appropriate for local circumstances and resources is crucial to success. The Nordic model is simply unsuitable for Papua New Guinea. The innovations of the 'package of benefits', the use of community leaders and local gathering places are all transferable ideas.

HIV/AIDS is one of the most pressing challenges to the health services of developing countries. Every three days someone in Barbados dies of AIDS. The real level of infection is almost impossible to calculate in the absence of random testing. The costs of treatment are very high. AIDS differentially affects women, who often have no means of preventing sex or requiring their partners to use condoms. Nor are some HIV infected women able to avoid breastfeeding (thus reducing child infections) because a stigma is attached to mothers who do not breastfeed. Often non-breastfeeding mothers are thought to be witches.

In the absence of effective safe sex education programmes, the main strategy of HIV prevention is to try to postpone sexual activity for as long as possible. However some girls have sex at seven years of age.

The discussion then widened to consideration of childcare, elder care, truancy and paternity. In developing countries the extended family may be the best institution for secure childcare and care of the aged. But the extended family is a metaphor for women who as mothers, wives, grandmothers and sisters are expected to supply care and nurturing.

Cultural Norms and the Bodies of Women and Girls

Later in the conference the impact of cultural norms on the health of women was again raised.

Germaine Greer, who argued that the practice was not well understood, took up the issue of female genital cutting in a strong and provocative statement. Opposition to female genital cutting often stemmed from a poor understanding of what it was, what it signified and how it was performed. The procedure takes many different forms. Moreover, opposition in the West was in some ways hypocritical. The practice of unnecessary hysterectomies, so common in the West, is a form of female mutilation. Female genital mutilation was raised at the first UN Women's Conference in Mexico City. Delegates thought that the African national representatives would be pleased but in fact they were offended. It might be unwise to condemn the practice because some groups might see it as an expression of their identity and it might also be a hidden form of resistance. More useful, she argued, to take measures to ensure the cutting is done in a safe way than to attempt to ban it.

Delegates were unconvinced by her arguments. It was pointed out that all forms of female mutilation and violence to women should be regarded as equally bad, wherever they took place.

Note

1 Based on the presentation by H. Elizabeth Thompson MP.

11 The Nordic model: the example of Finland[1]

The examples of Finland, Malaysia, Australia and the Caribbean offer insights into the scope and management of sex equality policy in different political and socio-economic environments. In the chapters that follow, each of these examples is outlined and discussed.

The UNIFEM (2000) report on the progress of the world's women stated that only Sweden, Denmark, Norway and Finland had achieved gender equality in secondary education, had reached the 30 per cent target for women in Parliament and had a gender balanced workforce. Nordic achievements are widely admired by women's rights advocates. The relatively favourable position of Nordic women is normally attributed to the strong economies, advanced welfare states and culture of equality in these countries. The great progress made by women since the 1970s is thought to be part of an integrated strategy in which a critical mass of women was achieved in each of the many public arenas. Critical mass may be defined as the number of women necessary in an organization to secure continuing presence of and sensitivity to women. Once achieved in a particular sector, critical mass enables women to perform critical acts on behalf of other women, thus beginning a virtuous circle in which the position of women continues to improve. Once achieved in one sector, critical mass tends to spread to other sectors. The experience of the Nordic strategy suggests important considerations about how to achieve sex equality, and offers a model that may be adapted to the conditions in other countries.

Of course the Nordic achievement is not one of unequivocal attainment of sex equality. Not only do the Nordic states contain many contradictions, but also many obstacles to full equality are still present. However, the achievement of equality in the Nordic states is an important political goal, regarded by policy makers as necessarily a continuous process. The case of Finland is an instructive example.

Equality between men and women may be defined in terms of its qualitative and quantitative dimensions. Quantitative equality may be measured in figures – in percentages, wages, and numbers. Quantitative indicators give some insight into how women and men compare in different areas of society and can show that there is (or is not) sex equality in work, pay, education, power and free time.

Qualitative equality has to do with the valuation by society of women's and men's skills, knowledge and experience. The use of the two kinds of equality indicators is very important because it captures the differences between women and men at the same time as ensuring their equality. Equality does not mean that women should be integrated into the workplace on men's terms; rather it suggests that women and men should be able to play an equal role and influence society, work and family life in their own way.

Nordic Policy

The Nordic countries promote *de jure* and *de facto* equality between women and men by mobilizing a number of different institutions. The cornerstone of sex equality is that women are economically independent. Accordingly very high numbers of Finnish women are employed outside the home, they are 50 per cent of the paid workforce, and mainly full time – part time work is exceptional in Finland. This high level of women's employment means that services are also geared to a model based on women working in paid employment outside the home. For example the basis of social security provision is personal and individualized, regardless of the family status of the recipient.

The notion of the working woman has been normalized in the Nordic countries in both rural and urban areas. Their centrality to the Labour market gives women a base in important areas of society. However, employment is to some extent sex-segregated, both vertically (whereby men are more likely to hold senior positions in a given occupation than women) and horizontally (whereby certain occupations are dominated by one sex or the other.) This phenomenon is normally called 'occupational sectoralization'. In Finland, the jobs mostly done by women are secretarial, clerical, teaching, nursing and service sector jobs. Male dominated jobs are in the building industry, the paper and metal industry, various technical areas and executive positions. Sixty per cent of working women work in professions in which women's share of employment is 80 per cent or more, in part a manifestation of the large welfare services sector. In common with the UK, Finnish unemployment in the 1990s was experienced more by men than women, a product both of occupational sectoralization and the different rates of unemployment in the service, primary and industrial sectors in a changing economy. By the end of the 1990s such sex differences had levelled off as sectoral adjustments took place.

The Nordic states are concerned about the extent of occupational sectoralization by sex and have taken measures to change it. Schools, for example, aim to interest increasing numbers of girls in mathematics and physics and increasing numbers of boys in nursing and other caring jobs. Project work and vocational guidance are the main methods used. There are signs of change. Finnish women are now better educated than are Finnish men; university educated women are more likely to do graduate work, for example.

Vertical segregation continues to be a problem. When educational statistics are compared with statistics on business executives and leaders, a huge gap is apparent. Despite their high educational achievements, women are only about 11 per cent of senior managers and about 25 per cent of middle managers. Mrs Tuulikki Petäjäniemi attributes this 'glass ceiling' effect to male resistance, meaning the bias men have in favour of other men. Strategies to change this bias include the maintenance of lists, or registers, of qualified women by the Equality Ombudsperson so that when positions are vacant, nominations of women can be made, thus countering the frequent charge that qualified women are not available. This strategy, also adopted in Denmark, can readily be used elsewhere. Mentoring is another strategy used to help promote women. Where an employee is judged to have career potential a career 'godparent' is appointed. The godparent becomes a career adviser, teacher and friend.

In the second part of her talk Mrs Tuulikki Petäjäniemi offered observations on policy challenges and achievements. She concentrated on four areas: equal pay, the reconciliation of work and family life, the role of legislation and the part played by women politicians.

Equal pay for work of equal value has not yet been achieved in Finland. The sum total of women's earnings is about 80 per cent of men's earnings. Horizontal sectoralization accounts for a significant amount of the gap, which is much smaller within occupational groups than it is in society as a whole. The jobs typically performed by women are less well paid than the jobs typically performed by men. Vertical sectoralization accounts for quite a lot of the remaining difference, as women often receive lower pay than men for the same work, particularly in the better-paid jobs.

Although the law is important, the achievement of equal pay cannot rest on legal change alone. Job evaluation schemes, particularly with collective bargaining arrangements in which women are full participants, are one of the most promising means of making advances to equal pay. Women's roles in trade unions therefore impact on their pay.

The reconciliation of work and family is now an objective in many countries. Finland has been a pioneer in constructing a service and aid network to assist parents of small children to combine work and family responsibilities. The cornerstones of such policies are childcare arrangements, job flexibility and maternal and parental leave arrangements. The priority given to childcare is evident from the fact that childcare continued improving even during the economic crisis of the 1990s. Parental leave may be used by either parent, is state funded for ten months, and may be continued unfunded for up to three years, after which the parent taking the leave is entitled to return to his or her old job. Both parents are entitled to an initial two weeks' leave. The majority of fathers use the initial leave, but only 7 per cent of those taking up the family leave are fathers. In addition, there is a prejudice against fathers who use their family leave rights. In Sweden and Norway policy makers are attempting to address this prejudice by encouraging men to take up careers as kindergarten teachers or in primary education.

Although legislation cannot by itself bring about sex equality, it is a central part of successful strategies. In Finland, the Act on Equality Between Men and Women came into being in 1987. This act aims to prevent sex discrimination and promote the status of women, especially in working life. It also applies to men, and men make about one-third of the complaints made under the act. An Equality Ombudsperson enforces the act. It requires employers to draw up equality action plans and to show progress in implementing it. Such schemes are successful provided they set realistic year on year achievable targets. Schemes that promise everything at once tend to fail and disappoint.

Political Women

Finnish women have a long history of political activity. They were second in the world (after New Zealand) to get the vote, and the first to win the right to stand as candidates for election. Women were present in parliamentary life from its beginnings, and now represent 37 per cent of MPs. The system for selecting candidates does not require quotas of women, although some political parties operate quotas. The electoral system is a proportional one, built on large multi-member districts in which voters are able to order candidates on lists according to preferences. This system is known to facilitate the election of women. Women's organizations in the parties play an important role in mobilizing women candidates and support for them once nominated.

Quotas do apply in the committees of the legislature, government and public appointments. Government, parliamentary and social committees and working groups, municipal organizations and so on are required to have at least a 40 per cent female membership. This model of public appointments is common in the Nordic states and has been discussed widely and often adopted elsewhere.

Another innovation is gender impact analysis. In the Nordic states all political decisions are, in theory at least, assessed for their effect on gender equality. Membership of the European Union has brought additional requirements of this kind.

The considerable political influence of Finnish women creates continuous pressure to bring women into leading positions in the public and private sector. Although the Nordic model has not yet delivered sex equality, it has established the virtuous circle necessary for that achievement. The Nordic model is founded on equal access to education and training, individual income and individual social security, the separate taxation of spouses and the provision of services to enable women to participate in working life. Its cornerstone is the economic independence of women.

Discussion

Much of the discussion of Finnish policy was about its technical aspects. The workings of the quotas, the details of funding candidates and the electoral system are all instructive examples of effective equality strategy. Eight per cent of state funding for parties was allocated to party women's leagues; this was often used to support women candidates.

There was also interest in the strategies to implement parental leave and to break down the barriers whereby caring work is typically done by women and less valued when men perform it. Some delegates were concerned that women's power would be reduced if they ceded control of child rearing to fathers. Others were concerned about the loss of status at work once a parent had been away for three years on parental leave. Retraining was often needed on return and patterns of working had often changed. Attention was also drawn to comparatively high rates of divorce in the Nordic states, the low birth rate and the high suicide rate.

Programmes to break down later discrimination by encouraging girls into scientific training were also discussed. Mrs Tuulikki Petäjäniemi acknowledged that it has proved difficult to get girls to train in mathematics and physics, and that breakthrough action plans were on the agenda. The increased need for workers with IT skills was likely to provide some of the demand necessary to attract women into technical occupations.

The powers of the Ombudsperson were detailed and Mrs Tuulikki Petäjäniemi noted that the media followed discrimination cases, providing an additional sanction. This is one of the many examples of the importance of a sympathetic, or at least balanced, media discussed at the conference.

Conclusion

Equality of employment is central to the Nordic model of gender equality. All Nordic countries have equality legislation, supported by ombudspersons who have the power to name and shame companies who fail to adhere to the programme. Achieving a balance between work and family is sought through systems of parental leave and flexible working and a social understanding that parenting is a shared responsibility. Although much has been achieved the workforce continues to be segregated by sex. To correct this, educational initiatives are being put into place.

Note

1 Based on the presentation by Mrs Tuulikki Petäjäniemi, Finnish Ministry of Labour, MP and former Equality Ombudsperson.

12 Equality policy: the example of Malaysia[1]

Between 1955 and 1999 the number of women in the Kuala Lumpur Parliament grew from one to twenty. This gradual change is thought to be continuing. However the rate of change will need to increase if the target for the achievement of equality between the sexes by 2020 is to be met. According to the national plan (Vision 2020), by this time the socio-economic infrastructure will support *de facto* sex equality. Meanwhile an elaborate and wide-ranging *de jure* policy has been devised.

The National Policy

The aim of Malaysian Government policy is to integrate women into the national development processes. Over the years administrative machinery has been established to accommodate women's needs. Initiatives include a Department on Women's Affairs set up in 1983. In 1983 the department was a division in the Prime Minister's Department, now it is a full department. A National Policy on Women was endorsed in December 1989 and formulated in December 1992. Its objectives are to eliminate all impediments and restrictions to the full integration of women in the development process. The policy is constructed around two main goals: first, to guarantee equitable sharing of resources, information, participation opportunities and benefits of development for both men and women, and second, to integrate women into all sectors of national development in accordance with their capacities and needs. The goal of equality and justice must be central to all development policies. In this context women will be able to enhance their quality of life, eradicate poverty, obliterate ignorance and illiteracy and ensure a peaceful, harmonious and prosperous nation.

The National Advisory Council on the Integration of Women in Development and the Women's Liaison Committees of the State Governments are responsible for the co-ordination of all the programmes pertaining to women. Various strategies to implement the policy include:

- relating issues to government administrative bodies through education and training
- strengthening the women/development machinery
- incorporating aspects of planning, implementation and supervision for women's integration programmes in the policies and actions of government agencies (gender mainstreaming)
- raising awareness of women
- encouraging the involvement of NGOs
- using affirmative action to eradicate inequalities
- supporting research programmes on women's issues
- providing adequate funding for equality programmes.

Women in Politics

Having outlined the national Sex Equality Framework, Rohani Binti Abdul Karim discussed the problems and opportunities for getting women into Parliament. Using research by the Inter-Parliamentary Union, she outlined the various channels of access to politics that women might follow, described the experiences of women running for Parliament, identified factors that made women reluctant to run for Parliament, and finally outlined ways to increase the representation of women in Parliament.

Channels of Access

The main channels of access to elected public office are political parties. However, party experience often combines with other public experience in qualifying a candidate for office. To succeed in political parties, women must learn and play by the rules. Therefore they must be able to demonstrate party loyalty, have proven political ability, and have worked actively in party organizations. In some political parties, affirmative action provides additional opportunities for women, perhaps shortening the long political apprenticeship that is often necessary to be considered for national public office.

Activity in NGOs and trade unions not only gives women experience of inequality and its legal and administrative implications, but also leads to an increase in political consciousness and visibility. In addition, leadership roles in NGOs and trade unions lead to wider community awareness and the development of important political skills. Certain professional careers are a particularly good training ground for politics, notably the law, teaching and government administration. Particular circumstances and sometimes luck (being in the right place at the right time) provide opportunities to be nominated. Family traditions, histories of activism, party participation, political commitments and passions, and peer pressures often assist women to seek political careers.

Experiences of Running for Parliament: The Barriers

Women face a number of difficulties and obstacles when running for Parliament. A number of common problems, fears and difficulties have to be overcome by women seeking office. Amongst women seeking office worldwide:

- 67 per cent struggle to balance the amounts of time they devote to private life and political activities.
- 37 per cent experience cultural values and attitudes that are hostile to women's participation in politics.
- 36 per cent experience financial problems.
- 31 per cent experience conflicts between their female identities and approaches and the demands of political life.
- 30 per cent lack a support network.
- 21 per cent have transportation problems.
- 20 per cent have security problems.
- 20 per cent dislike their experiences of the media.
- 19 per cent are ambivalent about becoming public figures.
- 16 per cent fear public speaking.
- 12 per cent have inhibitions *vis a vis* their constituents.

The Reluctance of Women to Run for Parliament

The reluctance of women to run for Parliament undoubtedly stems from the difficulties listed above. In addition, women's life circumstances and personal responsibilities inhibit their availability for public life. Cultural factors and the social construction of women as mothers make many women feel hesitant about candidacy. The reality of motherhood and family responsibilities relieves them of the opportunity to participate.

Increasing the Presence of Women in Parliament

General and specific factors can be adjusted to increase the representation of women in Parliament. General factors turn mainly upon social, cultural and attitudinal changes. Change is needed in community and cultural attitudes to women so that their participation in politics should be allowed to become the norm. Women should be encouraged to take greater interest and have greater knowledge of and involvement in political life. Practical ways to encourage equal sharing of household tasks with more men taking on family responsibilities would generate profound social change. At government and managerial level, gender planning will produce action and measures that take women's needs into account. For example, meetings might be scheduled at more convenient times for women, affordable day-care and childcare would release them from their family tasks for political participation. Good education and political training for women will increase their awareness of their political responsibilities and enhance their political interests. Public knowledge of the real work of politicians should be enhanced. More women role models and better publicity for existing women role models should facilitate the attraction of women to politics. Parliaments should encourage attendance by women, especially young women and girls so that they get a sense of parliamentary life. Induction programmes for newly successful women candidates would enhance their welcome and facilitate their parliamentary effectiveness. Schemes to finance aspirant women candidates on a cross-party basis might improve the willingness of reluctant parties to do more for political women.

Political parties are the keys to the enhanced parliamentary representation of women. The successful integration of women into Parliament requires real commitment and action by political parties. Parties should gender their candidate selection and recruitment practices, paying special attention to training in political skills, public policy issues and electoral institutions.

In conclusion, although social and economic improvement of their circumstances will enable more women to participate in politics, women will not achieve political equality automatically. Political leaders, women's organizations and the political parties all have a part to play in convincing the electorate to support women and in convincing women to come forward.

Discussion

Delegates were interested in the template for equality policy, but many pointed out the differences between *de jure* and *de facto* policies. Devising good policies is a challenge; more challenging is the process of implementation. Informal mechanisms were thought by some to be insufficient to bring about equality, others thought that informal mechanisms had as important a part to play as formal mechanisms, not least because so much of political life consists of customs and practices, implicit rules and informal agreements. The roles of NGOs both in mobilizing women and in mobilizing on women's issues are central to the process of achieving equality of representation. Different political approaches are necessary for different political circumstances. Malaysia with its eastern culture is not an appropriate site for the strategies that were implemented successfully in Scotland, for example. Gradual change in order to get people used to the idea of political women and working through traditional avenues in order to open up new channels for women are the foundation of Malaysian policy.

Note

1 Based on the presentation by the Hon. Rohanti Binti Abdul Karim MP.

13 The implementation of equal rights legislation: personal observations

Hon. Gillian James, MHA, Tasmania

Good design of equal rights legislation is a necessary but not sufficient condition for its success. Without adequate strategies for implementation and effective systems for monitoring and development the policy will fail. The Hon. Gillian James, Member of the House of Assembly in the Tasmanian Parliament, described the challenges of effective equality policy implementation. Her talk is reproduced in full below.[1]

What Can be Done to Ensure Equal Rights Legislation is Implemented?

To answer this question it is necessary to identify the reasons why it has taken so long to achieve the successful passage of legislation through respective parliaments in order to obtain even basic equal rights. Without the hard work, advocacy and driving force of women, equal rights legislation would not have come as far as it has. The legal, moral and social issues involved with differing political, legal and social interpretations of the complex concepts of discrimination, equality and equal opportunity have tended to limit the success of sex discrimination legislation. South Australia was the first state in Australia to pass legislation in 1975 and in my own state of Tasmania, after many attempts by my own Labour Party in opposition and in government, it took until 1995 to enact the Sex Discrimination Act.

In order to get legislation through both Houses of Parliament it was necessarily limited in its application. An amending Private Member's anti-discrimination bill covering wider grounds including race, social status, gender, sexual orientation, marital status, parental status, breast feeding, disability and trade union activity was passed through the House of Assembly in 1997 but did not receive the concurrence of the Legislative Council. It took an influx of women members in the Legislative Council and their considerable influence to result finally in the enactment of the Anti-Discrimination Act in 1998. Without the persistence and unity of women of differing political affiliations in both Houses this would not have happened. I think this emphasizes an important point that women can achieve a great deal by co-operating on such important issues.

The Australian Commonwealth Sex Discrimination Act 1984 (amended and consolidated in 1999) evolved over the intervening years since the Federal Parliament passed the original act. In 1969 the Commonwealth Conciliation and Arbitration Commission ruled that 'equal pay for equal work' was to be phased in by 1972. In 1972 the Commission extended the equal pay concept to 'equal pay for work of equal value', to be fully implemented by 30 June 1975. In 1973 Elizabeth Reid was appointed adviser to Prime Minister Gough Whitlam on matters relating to women, the first such position in the world. As long ago as 1983 Australia ratified the United Nations Convention on the Elimination of All Forms of Discrimination Against Women (CEDAW).

A House of Representatives Standing Committee on Legal and Constitutional Affairs' enquiry into equal opportunity and equal status for women in Australia led to the publication of its report entitled *Half Way to Equal*, in 1992. Consequently the provisions of the Sex Discrimination Act 1984 relating to sexual harassment were strengthened and the Act was extended to industrial awards. These examples demonstrate how difficult the path has been for dedicated individuals and governments to achieve the present equal rights legislation, which is still full of pitfalls and inadequacies despite Australia's ratification of CEDAW in 1983.

During that evolutionary period I have been politically and actively involved in various capacities and have certain observations to make. Exemptions from discriminatory legislation provisions in our jurisdictions are extensive and in many cases undesirable. It is my opinion that rather than exemptions being automatically allowable, any decision to apply an exemption or disallow one should rest on the merits of the case. As male attitudes, actions or lack of action are the main impediments to equal opportunities for women and minority or disadvantaged groups, they cannot be ignored. Men will listen, even be sympathetic and profess understanding, but unfortunately in many cases entrenched attitudes, peer group pressure and community attitudes influence them to act as follows. Either they do nothing to support equal opportunity legislation and its implementation, or they conservatively weaken the provisions aimed at assisting those who are being offended against. (However, in saying this, I am very much aware of the influence wives, partners and close female associates can have on men's thinking and actions.) This highlights the roles of advocacy, education and empowerment of women in achieving equal opportunity not simply for a selected few, but for all those who are not so empowered. Male politics is about wheeling and dealing, paybacks and payoffs, whereas women tend to put in the hard work or seek out a worthy cause first, and use logic and persuasion to achieve their aims. More can be achieved for both sexes if they are not diametrically opposed in their views and can move forward together for the benefit of both if there are no perceived threats to one another's aims and ambitions. This would mean a fair and equally represented society.

In this respect inclusiveness is all-important for mutual trust and must be the basis for sound equal opportunity legislation and its implementation. An Australian Senator, the late Pat Kennelly, is famous for a quotation, 'You take your logic, I'll take the numbers.' Unfortunately this is the way it has been happening in most parliaments throughout the Commonwealth and indeed the world, with women members in the minority. Despite moves for equal representation, this will not be achieved in the foreseeable future. Women therefore need to make men see the value of their aims in this and other social issues and get them to support them. All politicians are acutely aware of community attitudes and the potential effect on their respective careers. Where they need changing for the common good, women have to be at the forefront. Women are very good at networking, and international organizations such as ZONTA

International (of which I am a member), Business and Professional Women and Soroptomists, to name a few, are actively involved in advancing a wide range of women's rights issues. Locally the Women's Electoral Lobby, a non-partisan organization, has played a leading role in raising public awareness, as well as confronting Members of Parliament and candidates for election on matters affecting the well-being of women.

The concepts set out during the United Nations' World Conference on Women held in Beijing in 1995 adhere to the principle that 'human rights are women's rights and women's rights are human rights'. US First Lady Hillary Clinton stressed this principle at the Conference. No doubt the Beijing+5 Conference will reinforce those concepts and it is up to people such as you and I to see that they are carried through wherever possible.

It is not only women who suffer discrimination and less than equal opportunity and we must be mindful of this and fight against discrimination wherever it exists. The media has a role to play in exposing violence and discrimination rather than sensationalize, as it tends to do. There needs to be funding to ensure legal access where it is needed. Male dominated professions need to be challenged and women need to understand the masculine way of doing things, although not necessarily emulate them. The only criteria should be equality of performance. It has been said that whatever women do they must do twice as well as men to be thought half as good. Luckily this is not difficult. Women must have a high profile in their moves for equality (and certainly to have any chance of election to Parliament), but be not overbearing, perhaps subtle in order to achieve their aims. When a man perceives his dominance to be threatened, he tends to believe that offence is the best means of defence and react accordingly. As Members of Parliament we need to win the hearts and minds of fellow Members, Government, Opposition and in particular the bureaucrats to achieve just legislation and its administration.

We need to have their respect, be able to define clearly what it is we are about and communicate it to the community through our respective networks, local bodies, non-government organizations and at the 'grass roots' level. It is a big task, but communication and understanding should hasten the process.

To sum up, on matters such as the implementation of equal opportunity legislation and the resolution of associated social issues, women in power from all political parties need to unite as in many cases male dominance leads to a diminution of vital elements necessary for the effective administration of the law. Advocacy, lobbying, mentoring and the direct involvement of those with influence to bring about change are important in gaining social acceptance as well as awareness. These will bring about a change in negative public attitudes. Economic empowerment, networking and direct representation in the legislative process are important factors as is the winning of public opinion as there tends to be a widespread attitude of 'we put up with it, why don't they?'

Women don't look for sympathy but they need, expect and should have understanding and help when it is required from a community.

There is a different male perception of what equal opportunity means. As long as it does not pose a threat to them and their dominance, particularly in the workplace, then women can be equal, but in their view, not better. This leads to the 'glass ceiling' and the cutting down of 'tall poppies' syndromes. The Affirmative Action (equal Employment Opportunity for Women) Act 1986 (now known as Equal Opportunity for Women in the Workplace Act 1999) was passed by the Australian Federal Parliament, and in 1992 the Final Report of the effectiveness review of the Act was published and it called for a policy of contract compliance for those employers who fail to comply with the requirements of the Act. Contract compliance was subsequently introduced. Nevertheless women have been reluctant to complain, and with a move away from unionism there is a need for monitoring of compliance, perhaps by means of regular surveys.

Violence and poverty are two of the remaining barriers to true equality and it is important that we continue to work locally and globally to help remove these barriers. We also need to educate children to relate to and respect one another in order for women now and in the future to live without fear of discrimination or violence. I quote from the Reverend Martin Luther King Jr who said:

> One of the great agonies of life is that we are constantly trying to finish that which is unfinishable. But I can hear a voice

> crying in the vista of time saying, 'It may not come tomorrow, but it is well within thine heart. It's well that you are trying. You may not see it. The dream may not be fulfilled, but it is just good that you have a desire to bring it to reality.'

It is important that we should make every endeavour to have continuity of effort despite opposition and setbacks in order to achieve equality and justice for women and the undertrodden even if it takes what seems like forever.

CEDAW's policy recommendations need to be implemented as they cover most aspects of discrimination against women and I suggest that this (conference) calls on all governments and jurisdictions to make them mandatory. As an example we need to pursue the right to equity within our own Commonwealth Parliamentary Association, at the same time acting within our own sphere of influence. The Commonwealth Women Parliamentarians Group has come a long way in a relatively short time, but the movement for equality must continue and strengthen.

Discussion

Good implementation mechanisms and procedures are the mainstay of effective policy. Many countries have elaborate and beautifully structured policies as expressed in legislation, statements of aims and government manifestos, but their practices fall woefully short of the ideals so expressed. However, although progress has been made in sex equality legislation and policy, success has been disappointing when considered in relation to the aspirations of the founding legislation. Much has been learned in the thirty years or so since policies and policy machinery were first established. Education policy is of central importance to effective equal rights strategies. Women should be educated about their rights from a very early age. In many cases the judiciary also needed to be educated, particularly where equality principles had not previously been the subject of legislation. The importance of monitoring on the basis of good quality disaggregated statistics was widely affirmed and the importance of good channels of accountability for policy machinery repeatedly stressed. A sympathetic media that provided regular, balanced coverage of sex equality policies and progress was a major factor in implementing and improving policies. Some media offered annual lists of good companies to work for. A joined-up policy in which family and work were integrated was also crucial. Women's roles in the family, their responsibilities to children and others requiring care and their independent rights to property, income and so forth are fundamental principles of policy. Another principle that has had great success is contract compliance whereby government only made financial contracts with organizations that were gender balanced in both their staffing and provision and on the basis of good internal action plans to improve internal gender equity. To be fair, such gender balance needed to be calculated in terms of the relevant population, but this does not present insurmountable problems.

In summary implementation can be improved by encouraging the media to play a positive role, educating individuals about their rights, encouraging advocacy of women's rights by both sexes, mentoring and other forms of support for aspirant women, cross-party alliances of women and well designed policy machinery.

Note

1 Hon. Gillian James, AM MHA, 'What can be done to ensure equal rights legislation is implemented?'

14 Does size matter? Sex equality in small states[1]

Women have less access to the resources necessary for travel, but are thought to be better at the techniques of community. If so, then they might do better in small states where interactions are more likely to be face to face, than in larger states where other resources are necessary for participation. In his opening presentation to the discussion group on equity in small states, Mr Roy Bodden, MLA, considered recent changes in the status of women in the West Indies.

The background of slavery in the Caribbean left a legacy of matriarchy that had originated in the family structures and practices of ancient Africa and combined with European customs and practices to produce a particular matriarchate in slave society. Since the birth of the modern Caribbean in 1938 women have come to play a more public role. The Moyne Commission, convened following riots in the British Caribbean in the 1930s, indicated that Caribbean social development required changes in the roles of women and in expectations of women. Gradually women played a more active part in social and economic life and, in particular, became an important part of the trade union movement. However, the male dominated society of the British Caribbean did not accept women as political equals. The Second World War brought further changes of which a more participatory colonial relationship, the advancement of Crown/colony political relations and the spread of education were especially important. Widespread male suffrage led to universal adult suffrage. The vote was an accelerator of women's equity in the British Caribbean and probably of other small states there.

By the time adult female suffrage was granted, women already held important economic roles. With the vote they were, albeit grudgingly, accepted as partners. The acceptance of women as partners is, arguably, a very important part of liberation in a colonial society. But partnership is only one of several stages to equity. Women still have quite a lot to achieve in the Caribbean. They face considerable male resistance. Bodden noted that in the Cayman Islands women's ascent to equality with men and their entry into public life was a long and arduous process. The examples of spectacular achievements took place in a context in which unyielding men who were unwilling to concede extrafamilial roles to women begrudged political success for women. Such attitudes continue.

At the same time, and possibly as a result, the Caribbean women's movement is judged by Bodden to be relatively small and weak, not a player in the politics of sex equality.

In summary, a number of factors militate against the achievement of equality for women in smaller states. These include the continued male domination of important positions in the society, the reluctance of many women to give up their traditional roles, the mistaken conception that men are better suited to public life and the structure of many social organizations to have a built-in male bias. Caribbean society is not friendly to women either at work or in the family. Bodden concluded by stating his belief that it is up to women to change their circumstances and to create a dialogue that will break down the male dominance of public institutions.

Discussion

Sex equality policies must be designed for the circumstances in which they will operate. Cultural, economic and educational variations must inform the policy. Economic independence is normally a prerequisite for equity. To be successful equality programmes need to affect cultural attitudes. A rethinking process in society is needed so that an inclusive community is generated. Citizens must become aware of difference and realize that no one can afford to marginalize groups of the population. However, there are no general rules of procedure that will work in all circumstances. The size of a country does not matter.

Note

1 Based on the discussion paper by Roy Bodden, MLA.

15 How can NGOs lobby for change? A user's guide

Georgina Ashworth

Equality advocates play important roles in bringing about the changes that they seek. Their strategies may consist of lobbying decision-makers, or the provision of resources or the cultivation of a sympathetic media. The next three chapters are concerned with the techniques of advocacy (lobbying), the provision of micro credit and the politics of opinion change. Each chapter shows that change is most evident in circumstances in which women are present in decision-making, a point that is repeatedly made in discussions of women's representation.

For many years Georgina Ashworth has been active in NGO work, research, consultancy, writing and making change happen. Her reflections on her work and its lessons illustrate the elements of effective lobbying. The main resources of a lobbyist are knowledge, expertise and energy. The use of these resources is well illustrated in Georgina Ashworth's talk, which is reproduced below, followed by a summary of the ensuing discussion.

There may seem to be a contradiction between the solitary, thinking world of writing and the busy activity of lobbying, but I found it necessary to become active in lobbying to ensure that what I was writing about – making change for women in institutions and political structures – came about. The know-how I share with you is based on different successful experiences over many years, but always as an unpaid lobbyist, with commitment – not money – the motivation. I have not benefited personally from any of this lobbying.

It is useful to distinguish between advocacy and lobbying. Non-legal advocacy is a long-term, widespread activity of awareness raising and persuasion. It can perhaps be seen as a softening up for the more short-term, focused activity that is lobbying to make an actual change to a parliamentary bill or a UN document, or a policy, usually on a single issue. Both advocacy and lobbying need persistence and inventiveness, and the cases from Northern Ireland and Scotland at this conference are excellent examples of this.

To lobby you have to know the system and the subject well, the dates, the actors and the documents.

Knowing the system means finding out about the procedures, location, and access for NGOs and so on, and being clear about what you want to change. Therefore, you need to have done some fact-finding and research on both of these issues. It is very counter-productive to be vague or poorly informed.

You need to know the time-framework and the dates of the political process you want to influence and plan ahead according to how much you want to affect it. (Thus, for example, for the World Conference on Human Rights in 1993, which a number of us worked to make an impact upon, we identified the preparatory committee meetings, and worked for eighteen months overall in planning, drawing consensus from others, and finding the means to get there and the ways to put across our points.)

You need to know the actors, which means the (likely) supporters of your issue, the opponents, and those who are indifferent but might be swayed either way. It is not enough to know who your supporters are, because the arguments of opponents can be powerful. If you can you watch their voting behaviour on other issues, as in the case of MPs in parliaments or government delegations in international conferences; it is useful to follow their language and interests and keep a record of these. You can lobby officials or civil servants, either when they are acting as negotiators, or because they can pass your ideas on to their political bosses, or write them into a speech or a plan of action and so on.

You need to know the bill, or draft document you want to affect, very well, and to be precise about where you want insertions or deletions, with paragraphs by number and so on. All these should be written down, using the formulas that the negotiators use. You also need alternative/back-up language when your proposals are rejected.

It is useful to have arguments to support your proposals. These can consist of moral arguments (for instance, eliminate discrimination; meet states' obligations) but they should also include the benefit to the state, to the general public, and to men from the adoption of the measure or language. Economic benefits are particularly helpful. Arguments can also be supported with well-researched and compiled data and comparisons with other countries (so as to prove it is possible to put the measure into effect) and legal arguments from international human rights instruments that the country has ratified.

Good lobbying does need human resources – it is difficult to do alone – and it is therefore important to build the capacity of others, their speaking abilities, presentation skills and know-how, and then they can not only share the long, tiring exertions of lobbying, but also back you up and show that you are not alone. International lobbying teams prove an issue is not 'just Western' and therefore dismissible. Ensuring that the lobbyists are consistently well informed and polite is important for the reputation of the cause. Mutual support also helps you deal with the psychological impact of failure, success or postponement.

Failure means you have to deal with disappointment and frustration, and decide whether you can try again in another way, on another day. (Failure can be used for a media campaign, for instance: 'Bigots defeat women'.)

Success means dealing with your ideas being adopted, but for no reward. The lobbied are not always grateful, because success might mean you would come back to bother them again. Success can also leave you a sense of anti-climax and emptiness, without the activity that occupied your mind and time for a long time. Postponement means you will have another opportunity, but you may not have the resources to 'hang in'; you have to find a way.

Lobbying requires persistence and inventiveness, and the capacity to move quickly, responding to events. It is possible to have a concurrent campaign with media sensations, gimmicks and so on, or public awareness advocacy, but the lobbyists need to concentrate on their work, and the publicists on theirs. The activities are complementary – and some people are good at one, and not at the other: it is a good idea to do what you are best at.

Discussion: How Can NGOs Best Lobby for Change?

Lobbying takes place in different political environments; therefore it must always be purpose designed.

A good example is the League of Women Voters in Kenya, where only 8 of 210 MPs are women, and it will take too long for a critical mass to grow to make changes from within. The League has drawn together other like-minded organizations and they work together, to be both strong in numbers and to demonstrate that the issues are not those of a single group. They learned from a previous failure when an Affirmative Action Bill was rejected out of hand, and invited groups of male MPs to lunch to explain why the measures needed to be adopted, and this has proved successful. Now the Attorney General who asks for their expertise consults them, and they are drafting an Equality Bill on his behalf.

NGOs vary in the different legal frameworks in which they operate and the different ways they are financed. The term NGO covers a range of organization and activity, from community-based groups or organizations, to service providers, to professional associations, to single-issue campaign groups. Most countries have laws or codes of practice under which NGOs register, report publicly on their finances and staffing and so on; some governments control them whereas others expect them to be critical on behalf of those who they represent.

Funding arrangements were discussed at length. In the case of Canada, funding is given to registered NGOs by government, both directly and through special funds (for example, from 5 per cent of the revenue of casinos). Canadian NGOs are able to criticize government. In other countries government funding for NGOs is available only for the provision of services to the public in place of state bodies. In many countries, NGOs have difficulty securing funds and have to look to trusts or donor agencies, often in competition with one another. Fundraising is complex and time-consuming. (But there are some NGOs who seem to have privileged access over others to those who provide funding.)

NGOs often work in the community. This bottom up approach does not contradict the work of lobbyists because it generates the mobilized support necessary to underline arguments for change.

In summary, lobbying is an important activity. Although mainly focused at the top of the decision-making system, it derives credibility and legitimacy from work at the grass roots level. NGOs are able to use traditional lobbying strategies in their work. Civil servants and MPs need lobbyists because of their expertise and contacts with the community.

16 Improving access to credit, technology and business resources

Bowen Wells MP (UK House of Commons) led a working group on the improvement of women's access to credit, technology and business resources. The group agreed on the importance of micro credit schemes as pioneered by Professor Yonnus of the Bank of England. Such schemes are available to 300 million low-income women. They are designed to enable women to set up or expand micro businesses. One of the most important lessons of implementing the scheme was that women quickly learned to work together in groups to support each other financially. That co-operation often led to their working on social issues relating to the education of children, the problems of violence, unfair discrimination and access to resources.

The group supported the UNICEF view that micro credit must be joined to access to basic social services such as health care, education and adequate nutrition for women and their families. Schemes to provide basic human rights education, literacy programmes and broader strategies to remove structural barriers to women's development should operate alongside the provision of small loans and savings incentives.

Micro credit schemes are of variable quality. As they grow in volume government should take measures to prevent fraud and to prohibit usurious interest rates and management charges. Lower cost mechanisms are needed to enable graduation from micro finance into the mainstream of financial services. It was agreed that the best way to nurture and develop successful small businesses was through the provision of Business Nursery Centres in which the spirit of co-operation and mutual support would continue and specialist services such as marketing, financial and accountancy support could be offered at affordable cost.

It was observed that there were many women who were not interested in managing their own enterprises. Many women would continue to depend for their advancement on the expansion of employment opportunities in companies operating in the textile industry, tourism, agriculture and other businesses. Employment would give them the independence of their own income in addition to that of their husbands. Experience of independence would enable them to graduate to responsible supervisory positions. It is important that the WTO presses on to a Development Round of trade regulation in spite of the debate at Seattle in 2000. In some countries employment opportunities continue, with education to enable women to move into the information technology sector, including the processing of computer data and the provision of financial information and services.

Such opportunities are available only to a minority of poor or relatively poor women. In developing countries, 200 million girls still do not have access to education, despite efforts to increase women's literacy. The literacy gender gap in developing countries continues to widen. Of the 1.3 billion people in the world who survive on less than one US dollar per day, 910 million or 70 per cent are women. Of this 70 per cent, almost half (450 million) live in India, another 14.8 million live in Pakistan and up to 30 million in Bangladesh. Until the underlying women's poverty is addressed gender discrimination in access to education, health services, credit, inheritance rights, technology and business resources will continue. Although schemes facilitating access are having significant effects on women's social and economic status, they are available to only a small minority. The work needs to be expanded if the eradication of women's poverty and disadvantage is to be a realistic goal.

17 Can the media be re-sexed?[1]

Jackie Ashley

Sex equality advocates have long understood that the print and broadcasting media have a significant part to play in bringing about equality of women and men in public life. The role of the media features in the PfA. Delegates who, on the whole, did not feel that the press played a positive role, frequently discussed its responsibilities. Many delegates expressed real despair about inappropriate and sexist media representations of women and some argued it was a waste of time to try to change the media. When British journalist Jackie Ashley described her experiences of the British national press and broadcasting she confirmed that there was still quite a long way to go. However she considered that some achievements had been made. Thus, while some of her experiences are far from encouraging to those who believe the media have a responsibility to present and treat women fairly, she was able also to report significant changes. Her talk is reproduced below.

Before I start, I'd like to say that I have doubts about the title of this paper. 'What can the media do to promote the interests of women?' seems to imply that the media want to help women generally and women in public life in particular. I'm not sure that's true. Perhaps a better title would have been 'How the media make life extremely difficult for women in public life and which editors should be locked up in the Tower of London'.

Newspapers

The media always was, and still is, male dominated, in both personnel and in outlook. We do at last have some women editors:

Rosie Boycott at the *Daily Express*, Janet Street-Porter at the *Independent on Sunday*, Rebekah Wade at the *News of the World* and in Scotland, Rebecca Hardy at *The Scotsman*. These women have made a difference.

At the *Daily Express* Rosie Boycott has managed to introduce a much more feminized agenda to a fairly recalcitrant news desk: the paper, as well as changing its political tone, carries many more stories now about health, adoption, education and crime from a woman's perspective. A woman, Ros Wynne Jones, is now one of their chief roving reporters covering the world's trouble spots and famines. Despite furious complaints from some old *Daily Express* readers, the strategy has proved successful, and the *Daily Express* is starting to gain readers at last. This is a real example of where a woman editor has managed to change the culture of a newspaper.

There are other encouraging signs: women journalists have started to network. In the past, male journalists would meet up at the Garrick or some other such London club, and hand out the top jobs to each other. Now there is a network of women who talk to each other, and bring other women into certain areas of the papers: there are political columnists like Polly Toynbee of the *Guardian* and Alice Miles of *The Times*, as well as business editors, media editors and of course consumer and fashion editors.

But there are still key areas that are virtually no-go areas as far as women are concerned. Most news desks remain male dominated, and therefore so are the papers' agenda. The large majority of political correspondents, and certainly political editors, are male, as are most leader writers and writers on public policy. Women are still more likely to be writing columns such as 'What I think about my Sainsbury's trolley', than they are to be giving an analysis of the Budget.

So, does this continuing absence of women at the top matter? Of course it does, particularly if we care about democracy. If women are not represented in the media, the media will carry a distorted view of society and of public life. A recent survey by the pressure group Women in Journalism showed that newspapers are out of step with real women's lives. They concluded that the way newspapers use images of women is at best old-fashioned and at worst complacent.

Their research began with the understanding that there are more men than women in public life; that women transgressing accepted social and moral codes are deemed more newsworthy than male transgressors, and that a premium is placed on a woman's appearance in industries such as show business and advertising. But, they said, more women work now than ever before, more women are making an impact – at all levels up to and including the boardroom – and there are more women MPs. Women in Journalism tracked editorial coverage in nine national dailies over a four-week period last autumn. It found that while women make up just under half of the total readership, they are significantly under-represented in photographs in national newspapers – just 20 per cent, yes, that's even with those infamous page three pictures in the *Sun* newspaper – compared with nearly 60 per cent of men. And they found, not surprisingly, that men are more often pictured in serious roles than women. Most papers, they concluded, failed to reflect the diversity of modern women's lives. For as long as the media aren't reflecting life as it is for women, it's going to be difficult to make further progress.

Then there's the issue of what's covered – what's of interest to women. The *Daily Mail* – which spends a good deal of time and money targeting women – has a fairly uncompromising stereotype of women: they are the victims of terrible crimes – stories abound of rape and assault; they feel guilty about being working mothers; they are fairly stupid about matters of economics and public finance, and suffer a good deal of back pain for which they are constantly looking for a cure. Well, the *Daily Mail* is right in one respect: women, it seems, do have different priorities.

A pamphlet published by the Fabian Society, written by the Labour MP Harriet Harman and Deborah Mattinson of Opinion Leader Research (a polling organization), has found that women do see their politics differently from men. They're less impressed with statistics and public announcements, taking their views more from their direct experience of things like schools and hospitals. They're more impatient for delivery of government promises: they don't like abstract discussions and they do like concrete facts. As with politics, so with the media: the media is the filter through which women see their politics, and the way it's presented doesn't seem to be very relevant to their lives.

According to Deborah Mattinson's research, politics is seen by women as a male pursuit, a gladiatorial game, not suited to women's personalities. We have a chicken and egg situation here: is politics presented by the media as an exclusive male preserve because it is so, or is the fact that politics is seen to be a male preserve what puts a lot of women off going into public life in the first place?

Women certainly require a far thicker skin than men if they are going to step into the limelight. I'd like to read to you the way in which a group of male sketch writers described Patricia Hewitt, Minister for E-commerce, and a rising star among the new intake of Labour MPs – tipped for the Cabinet before too long.

This dates back to a Treasury question time last year when Ms Hewitt was economic secretary, and was answering questions. A woman minister answering questions was not exactly unheard of, but it was the first time Patricia Hewitt had come to the attention of the political sketch-writers. So here's Tom Sutcliffe of the *Independent*:

> Patricia Hewitt adopts the role of a veteran nursery school teacher – a woman who thinks of herself as having a special way with the little ones. The ghastly singsong in which she delivers New Labour's bedtime story is accompanied at all times by a fixed smile, an acknowledgement that you need lots of patience if you're going to work with toddlers.

Then we have Matthew Parris from *The Times*:

> Ms Hewitt, in whom I am having increasing difficulty in believing, wore an eau-de-nil silk blouse with mega-shoulders, and radiated glitter-quality. You could imagine her stepping from a stretched white Cadillac. And she addressed MPs in the most extraordinary manner. It took this sketch writer back to infancy, watching a 1950s children's television programme called *Rag, Tag and Bobtail* and hearing *Listen with Mother* on the BBC.

And not forgetting Quentin Letts in the *Daily Telegraph* who wrote of the:

> Utterly ghastly, nannyish Patricia Hewitt. Urrgh, it's hard to convey how infuriating Miss Hewitt is. Properly to comprehend, you need to hear her pitying tones, her creepy, syllable-by-syllable enunciation, her are-we-all-sitting comfortably delivery.

Followed by Simon Hoggart of the *Guardian*:

> Ms Hewitt addresses MPs as if they were nice middle-class children. 'Ask Daddy to give you one of his empty Chianti bottles', you expect her to say. She was wearing a shiny metallic eau-de-nil jacket, so she looked like a sales rep's Mondeo.

All sound a bit familiar? I'll let you into the secret of how the honourable members of the press, Her Majesty's sketch-writers, conduct themselves. A brief half hour in the chamber of the House of Commons, and they repair to the press gallery cafeteria for tea and crumpets – in Quentin Letts' case, I imagine it's lots of crumpets. And there they chat around what they've seen and try to think up the day's image together, and who they're going to go for in print the next day. If ever a female MP's been speaking, it's easy. After all, women don't usually wear dull grey suits, with dull grey hair styles to match and they don't speak in dull grey tones. So they'd decided – to a man – to mock Patricia Hewitt – a sensible and hardworking MP – not for what she said, but for the way that she said it, and of course the way she looked.

Nanny Hewitt was the theme of the day. Then it's just a question of which of them can devise the cleverest twists on the old yarn.

It wasn't a one-off. Only last week the ever-so-witty Quentin Letts was having a go at another two women, Angela Browning and Helen Liddell. Angela Browning –'beaky Mrs Browning' he calls her – has, according to Letts, 'a high decibel voice so tonally astringent that it could cut through whale fat'. The exchanges between Mrs Browning and the industry minister Helen Liddell had poor MPs wincing, according to Mr Letts, 'as the two women shrieked at each other. Eventually, the Speaker had to bawl "Order", to silence the two wailing banshees.' All very funny – but actually what Quentin Letts was mocking was not two politicians, but two women. Yes, women do have higher voices than men; they tend to be born with them. But every time a woman speaks in public she's accused of wailing or shrieking – or worse.

So it's a brave woman who'll go into politics in the first place. The largely male Westminster lobby considers them fair game from the very start. Patricia Hewitt is not alone. Look at the way the pack hurrahed after Harriet Harman when she was in the Cabinet, pursuing her with all the enthusiasm of a pack of hounds in pursuit of their prey, and ripping her guts out once she was down. Mo Mowlam hasn't fared much better. Her gutsy manner, and her brave battle against a brain tumour, made it harder for the press to attack her. But then she became too popular – more popular than the Prime Minister possibly, so then it only took a few of those evenings where male politicians and spin doctors share a few jars with male journalists for the story to emerge that – sadly, following her illness – Mo was a few pence short of the full shilling now. She was, in a word, dispensable. The male establishment, through a few carefully planted stories, managed to undermine this unusual and charismatic politician. It took only a few weeks of the steady drip, drip of diary comments for even allies of Mo Mowlam at Westminster to be asking: 'What is it with Mo – has she really lost it?'

In her study of the new Labour MPs, published in a book called *Westminster Women* in 1998, the journalist Linda McDougall reported that nearly all those she spoke to felt that the press treated women MPs differently from men, and they all wished it was not so. She quotes the junior minister Angela Eagle and her twin sister Maria, also an MP, the pair of them very far from frivolous, being written about under a headline, 'New Labour, New crumpet'. Then there was Maria Fyfe, contacted by the *Sun*, not for an interview about her politics but to ask if she'd have her picture taken with a rose in her hair, or better still, held in her teeth. The sex lives of women MPs have of course a seemingly endless fascination for the popular press. Joan Ruddock, MP, the former Labour Minister sees it as the press's response to women's attempts for more equal representation: 'Newspapers investigating women politicians tended to go tangentially at that person as a woman and to use a particularly sexist technique ... diminishing her as a political figure.'

Can it change? Only, I believe, when women journalists start to storm the bastions right at the heart of newspapers. One senior female political journalist confided to me recently that she had nothing but contempt for many of her male colleagues at Westminster: 'they're chauvinist and ignorant', she said. 'The way they talk about women is simply Neanderthal.' But she recognized that as long as she was in the minority – often the only woman journalist in a gathering – she wasn't going to be able to change the tone of the conversation, and therefore of the reporting. There's a long way to go before the majority of male journalists even begin to take female politicians seriously.

The parliamentary lobby, like most newsrooms, is dominated by football-loving lads, whose priorities are very different to those of the majority of women. Even the so-called left-wing press is not immune. A few days ago Tessa Jowell, one of the Ministers for Women, had a long conversation with a journalist – who shall remain nameless – from the *Observer* newspaper. He talked for some half an hour about the projects she was involved with, from extending the New Deal to widening choice in childcare. But at the end of it all he was very excited about just one small part of her portfolio: the seminar she's holding this week on women's body image. It's a serious attempt to win over magazine editors and fashion journalists to the cause of big is beautiful – or at least, you don't have to look like Kate Moss to be fashionable – to try to counteract the dramatic rise in eating disorders among young people. But the *Observer* journalist's response was all too typical: 'Yeah, fat girls wanting to be thin – great pictures – that's just the kind of story we want.' Another excuse to festoon their pages with semi-naked pictures of women's bodies.

The Women in Journalism study found that most women working on national newspapers were faced with the constant dilemma over the use of images of women. Male executives are always more eager to use pictures of women, but the motivation behind this – and the criteria used in selecting those images – can be questionable. In all, the written press seems to be some years behind society as a whole on the matter of women's involvement in both the workplace and in public life. How quickly, if at all, the press will change is a matter for debate.

The Broadcasters

I want to turn for a few moments to broadcasting – the area of the media where I've spent much of my professional life, as a political correspondent for ITN for twelve years, and now a political programmes presenter for the BBC and London Weekend Television. Here the picture is more encouraging: there's a far greater awareness of the need for a balanced team – after all, on screen, there's no hiding the fact that there's no woman in sight – and far less tolerance of the traditional chauvinist attitudes. Things have changed quite quickly. When I was first pregnant, twelve years ago, having only recently been promoted to my post as political correspondent, I announced the news to my colleagues and waited for the congratulations. It was a long wait. The response from the male news editor was 'Silly ... Why doesn't she get rid of it? Does she need the address of a good clinic?' That, I believe, would simply not happen now. Television and radio have employed a good number of women reporters over the last ten years, and of course, a good many of them have become pregnant. Both the BBC and ITN have led the way in allowing job shares and flexible working – though there is still some way to go.

There remains though, a degree of tokenism about the employment of women, and the use of women in programmes. As long as there's one, goes the theory, then it's okay. So programmes like *Question Time* and *Any Questions* will always have one token woman, but it's not often they have a majority of women. Then there is the discrimination that still exists against older women: you can probably count on the fingers of one hand the number of older women who are seen regularly on television. It's as if they don't exist, they've been airbrushed out of the political debate. So while newsreaders such as Michael Buerk, Peter Sissons and Trevor MacDonald are thought to have gravitas and bottom with their grey hair and grizzled faces, women of the same age, like Julia Somerville and Carol Barnes, are quietly retired, or sent off to the radio where the lines won't show. Having passed the magic 40 myself, I'm well aware that my days on television are probably numbered.

So, that's how it is: what can the media do to help women? If it wanted to, I believe the media can do an awful lot. But it's only going to if there's pressure on the male establishment to change. Just as it became unacceptable to put out a programme or a panel without one woman, so we need to work towards an acceptance that the token woman isn't enough. There are always going to be more men in the workplace and in public life than women because of women's child-rearing duties; but the old ways of seeing the public debate dominated by men with a few younger women thrown in for light relief must be over.

The media could start by recognizing that forgotten group, the older women – WI woman if you like. For those of you from overseas, British prime minister Tony Blair was given the bloodiest nose he's had in his political life two weeks ago by 10 000 ladies from the WI, the Women's Institute, when he addressed them in a patronizing way with a party political speech. The women slow-handclapped, and some even walked out, leaving the prime minister looking more discomforted in public than he's ever done. That one event has done a lot to put older women back on the political map. Suddenly the media and the pollsters are aware that these women exist and that they can be a political force. Let's hope the momentum doesn't fade away.

The media could also accept that men and women do things differently – and not always assume that the male way is the right way. If men are more combative and forceful in debate, it doesn't always mean that they're right. Women are less confrontational, more inclined to negotiate, but it doesn't mean their point of view has any less validity. An interesting new book called *The Sexual Renaissance* by Sue Tibballs suggests we need a new approach to the gender debate. Instead of pushing feminism, she argues, we need to take account of the fact that 'the majority of people feel deterred by what they see as an out of date ideology'. Five years ago the think-tank Demos conducted some research that found:

> The backlash, which took hold against feminism in the 1980s, continues in the 1990s with a younger generation of women being as susceptible to negative images of feminism and feminists as older women. Young women still see it as extreme, man hating and extremist.

Well, so too do the media, so Sue Tibballs suggests a redefinition of the gender issue. Instead of pursuing absolute equality, she maintains that men and women are different, and that:

> Now that women have secured a legal and democratic status more equal to men, and begun to participate more fully in society, the differences between the sexes in how they live and think, and the social and cultural conditions of that difference have come to the fore … it becomes easier to see how each sex brings distinct male and female approaches.

That seems to make sense to me: to stop seeking absolute equality, but to admit there are gender differences and to celebrate them. Am I therefore advocating a return to the old days when news was for men, and women had their Women's Page with knitting patterns and recipes? Certainly not. But what I think this new approach does mean is that women in the media should be free to be themselves. It's reported that some of those who make it to the top – like Rebecca Hardy at *The Scotsman* or Bridget Rowe, formerly editor of the *Sunday Mirror* – are even more macho than the blokes they replaced. Perhaps they feel the need to prove that they've got balls too. This doesn't need to be the case. Women do things differently and should be allowed to do so. But this will only happen when they are not in such a minority in the media as they are now.

I haven't yet mentioned the very key subject of working hours. The media is known for its excessively long working hours – the very idea of a forty-eight hour week is treated as a joke – often it's more like a forty-eight hour day. And until that changes, women will, as has happened to so many of my female colleagues, jump off the career ladder and go freelance. It simply isn't possible to work the kind of hours demanded by many jobs in both the press and broadcasting, with the unsocial hours too, if you have a family, especially a young family. Freelancing is a very attractive option for women with children: the work can usually be fitted in around the demands of school runs, piano lessons, teatime and the like. But the problem with the majority of women freelancing is that they then don't make it into management. And that brings us back to where I started. The lack of women at the top of journalism must have something to do with the hours they have to put in. Work–life balance is the subject of many a feature in the press, but few journalists have actually put it into practice in their own lives.

Even this New Labour Government, which is in theory committed to improving the work–life balance, seems to take the issue with a large pinch of salt. A few days ago I was having dinner with a New Labour couple – Tony's cronies if you like. He works in Downing Street, she has an arguably even more important and demanding job. She was complaining that he leaves home every morning by 6.30 to rush into the office, leaving her to sort out the children. 'What about your work–life balance?' I asked him. 'That's all very well for other people, but not for me', he replied. 'I'm just too busy.' Which sums it up: everyone is too busy to achieve a work–life balance, and until the government really starts to encourage it, nobody is going to do anything other than pay lip-service to the idea.

I'm straying away now from what the media can do to help women, but actually I think the media won't do very much unless there are more women up there to change it. The media will always chase women readers and viewers, but that's the extent of their interest in the subject of equality. Perhaps progress will continue to be incremental – a little advance here, a little step forward there. For almost every woman who does become a programme editor, a section editor or a political editor, there's a pyramid benefit for women – both in terms of her encouraging others, and in the coverage and use of women in stories covered. It's taken us a long time to get this far. Let's hope that for our children's generation, conferences like this don't even need to take place – and it's no longer necessary to point the finger at those editors who need locking up in the Tower of London.

Discussion

In Britain, the increase in the numbers of women MPs in the House of Commons has had a good effect on the experiences of women in the lobby. However, the biases and blinkers of press coverage continue. Moreover, the way that politicians play the media may be sexist and obfuscatory. One delegate reported a national leader who always affirmed the need for the advance of women in his speeches in English; but when speaking in his own language he said that women must stay at home. Journalists around the world are not interested in women's issues, and are much less likely to give them coverage than other issues. Most delegates felt that such responses were the result of male dominance of the press and broadcasting media. Although we should bear in mind that few politicians, if any, are satisfied with their media coverage, such acceptance should not blind us to gender biases and outright sexism in media reporting, dissemination of images and employment policy.

Note

1 Jackie Ashley addressed the session on the media.

18 Conclusions

Rosie Campbell

The under-representation of women in public life is to varying extents a feature of all contemporary societies. However, a women-centred perspective can fail to address the complexity of the ways policy, legislation and economic and political forces impact on the lives of women and men. By contrast, a gender perspective can facilitate detailed and targeted policies to specific national arenas without sidelining the continued emphasis on the need for equal access to public life. In line with the Beijing and Beijing+5 process, a human rights approach can provide the framework for legislation. In this sense women's rights should be understood as human rights and women's concerns as human concerns.

The past twenty years have seen major developments in the collection and dissemination of accurate statistics regarding the position of women in society, which in turn has contributed to the development of a commitment for change. For example, the 1991 Harare Declaration, adopted by Commonwealth Heads of Government, identified several priority areas for the Commonwealth, including 'equality for women so that they may exercise their full and equal rights'.

Commonwealth and other international initiatives, coupled increasingly with measures for monitoring and evaluation, have helped create an enabling environment whereby women's non-participation in decision-making fora is now universally recognized 'as a democratic deficit'. All participants supported the target set by Commonwealth Heads of Government in 1997 of no less than 30 per cent of women in decision-making in the political, public and private sectors by the year 2005, but a recurring theme of the conference was that men still hold the overwhelming majority of national decision-making positions, in both the Commonwealth and worldwide.

The UNIFEM biennial report (2000) on the progress of the world's women stated that only Sweden, Denmark, Finland and Norway had achieved gender equality in secondary education, reached and exceeded the 30 per cent target for women in Parliament, and had a workforce containing 50 per cent women. Progress has not been strictly in line with economic resources and many developing countries have, with political will, surpassed the representation of women in public life achieved by some developed nations. Gender inequalities are not evenly distributed within nations, with women in some countries enjoying equal opportunity in employment but no or little opportunity for women to participate in politics by either voting or standing for election. The subtle differentiations in gender balance highlight the need for a country-specific approach while at the same time acknowledging common features of inequality. Some argue that Western countries should resist the temptation to perceive themselves as superior in the realm of women and public life, and should look at their own practices before condemning others.

Political parties and governments commonly claim to possess the political will to chose female candidates, but maintain that there are insufficient suitable women to choose from. In many cases empirical examples demonstrate that this is untrue. For instance, the political parties in Northern Ireland made this claim, but once the women's coalition appeared to be a real threat to their position, suitable women were quickly found. However, there is a need for institutions to be assessed with regard to gender. Parliaments are masculine institutions and adversarial, aggressive and confrontational political styles can create an inhospitable environment for women. In order to address the masculine nature of parliaments, sitting times and arrangements (horseshoe, adversarial or in the round) need to be considered, alongside the provision of facilities such as washrooms and childcare, or crèches, in order to provide a women-friendly and family-friendly working environment.

Female politicians can employ strategies to help provide support networks for women MPs and to mobilize a pool of women available for political parties to select as candidates. This support may be found and created within women's arms of political parties and can take the form of internal or external networking. External methods should include working across party lines on common issues, as well as interactions with other bodies. Mentoring schemes can be established with particular individuals or groups and female politicians can address women's organizations, trade unions or professional associations. This has the dual effect of providing support and interaction for women MPs, allowing them to connect directly with women's concerns, as well as encouraging qualified women to consider standing for Parliament. Female politicians should also attempt to develop a positive relationship with female journalists and broadcasters, because the male dominated nature of the press can distort images of women MPs and politics as a whole, which discourages women from becoming involved in politics.

The efforts of female politicians will not alone guarantee the equal access of women to Parliament. It is important for advocates to emphasize the fact that the political selection procedure of many parties does not provide a level playing field. This imbalance can justify the use of quotas as temporary measures to create a critical mass of women, who will be able to bring women's issues into the mainstream of political debate and 'feminize' Parliament. There is often a fear that women candidates who are selected through special measures will become part of a two-tier system. However, this depends upon the quality of the candidates. Training is therefore required for potential female candidates, and political parties must be prepared to fund these programmes along with gender-sensitizing training for all candidates if equal representation is to be achieved. Parties must also put women candidates in winnable seats. Proportional representation electoral systems can help to bring about the equal representation of women.

While training and special measures directed at professional women and parliamentarians can help to address the imbalance in parliaments, the inequalities in society that contribute to this imbalance must be tackled if long-term goals are to be met. Initiatives must be targeted at the grass roots and at the earliest stages. Educational programmes such as Youth Parliaments help to instil democratic values in young people and when girls and boys are involved in equal numbers they can achieve a common sense of self confidence in their ability to speak publicly and voice their opinions.

Educational programmes are needed to change social values and help women overcome the problem of balancing their traditional domestic roles with public life. If more women are to enter public life, more men must participate in the domestic sphere. Some argue legislation is often required to alter long-term societal and cultural traditions that create barriers for both women and men. Legislation of this type can be used to enforce equality measures, such as women's right to own property, or it can ensure that girls and boys participate in the same activities, be it cleaning or sport. Measures to support progressive men who wish to take an active domestic role, such as paternity and parental leave, can alleviate some of the pressures that keep women out of public life, whilst emancipating men to have fulfilling relationships with their children.

In the resolution of conflicts women are often congratulated for their help in the peace process and then written out of the negotiations. Often women activists have to initiate grass roots action in order to influence the politicians. Women have to push for inclusion in the political process by applying both internal and external pressure. Women's issues are not side issues but constitutional issues, and as the victims of war women have a right to political representation. Female politicians can add a new, more co-operative and reconciliatory dimension to conflict resolution, and they should push for cross-party interaction and remove themselves from the rhetoric-based politics common in conflict situations.

Equality of employment is central to the Nordic model of gender equality, which is based on the idea that women demand equity and not merely formal equality. The Nordic countries have equality legislation, which is supported by ombudspersons who have the power to name and shame companies who fail to adhere to the equality programme. Achieving the right balance between work and the family is achieved through the understanding that mothers, fathers and firms hold joint responsibility. Maternity, paternity and parental leave along with other measures such as flexi-time and unpaid leave help to facilitate equal opportunity of employment. However, the Nordic countries are not without their problems. The workforce is highly segregated and educational initiatives are being put in place to try to rectify this.

If an admissions officer is faced with two equally qualified applicants, the officer should choose the minority or female candidate. Such affirmative action interventions can supplement equality of employment programmes. While the need for affirmative action was generally recognized, most agreed that it was a temporary, partial and perhaps flawed remedy that needs to be accompanied by other measures.

Women constitute more than half of the world's human resources, and those firms and countries that make efforts to realize women's potential will benefit from increased competitiveness in the global marketplace. Some argue the processes of globalization and development can have a more negative impact on women than men. Women's domestic responsibilities make them immobile, and private enterprise has excluded women from full participation in the workplace. Initiatives to help women start small enterprises such as micro credit and business nurseries can counteract the destructive effects of gender blind policy. The success of the Grameen Bank in Bangladesh in providing small loans to women at the local level and improving their chances of escaping the poverty trap was highlighted as an example of good practice. Such initiatives should be accompanied by basic social services. Provision should be made for training and support for women who choose not to attempt to run small businesses and wish to work in expanding industries.

At the Fourth World Conference on Women in Beijing in 1995 it was agreed that there is a need to ensure women's full and equal access to training and education, with an emphasis on literacy. Two-thirds of the one billion illiterate people in the world are women and the literacy gender gap, partly because of demographics, continues to grow. It is therefore productive to link literacy training with other social education programmes, such as family planning and culturally specific practices. Education can be linked to local women's organizations, and it is helpful to tackle several issues simultaneously, for example by teaching mothers literacy with their children. Attempts need to be made to encourage women to enter male-dominated fields such as engineering, science and technology. Mentoring programmes and educational initiatives are needed to provide girls with the confidence to choose to enter male-dominated fields. Support networks should also be put in place to ensure that women are able to stay in these fields.

In education the necessity for gender mainstreaming is clear. In many countries, boys are underachieving in education, and a gender lens facilitates an approach, which is specific to the needs of boys as well as girls. Addressing male marginalization requires better male role models. Professional men should become involved with schools and educational projects. Initiatives to increase the numbers of male teachers are also useful. In the same way as it is necessary to look at school textbooks to remove gender biases that limit girls' expectations, where boys are underachieving it can be helpful to choose topics which are of particular interest to boys. It is interesting to note, however, that in those countries where girls are gaining better qualifications than boys, women are still under-represented in public life, and there is still a need for special measures to guarantee them access.

Women are denied equitable access to health care because of poverty and their lack of education, in conjunction with social mores that prohibit seeking treatment or intervention. When women are unable to perform their roles as mothers and caregivers, society suffers. Where access to care is dependent on finances, women are vulnerable because of their position in the workforce and the relationship between gender and poverty. Health education needs to take place at the community level, and involving community and religious leaders helps to overcome the problems of misinformation and ensures that the target audience is reached. As with education, health interventions for women can be linked to other events such as children's fairs or immunization programmes. Legislation can be a powerful instrument to effect change and when penalties are attached communities will respond.

In 1999 the global death toll from AIDS was 2.6 million and some 5.6 million more people became infected with HIV. In developing countries women constitute the highest risk group for the HIV/AIDS virus. In some countries married women cannot ask their husbands to use condoms yet male promiscuity is accepted. In some cases witch doctors prescribe unprotected sex with young virgins as a cure for the virus. These practices highlight the need for educational initiatives located within the community and for the need to educate community leaders themselves.

The Beijing+5 conference in New York in June 2000 discussed many of these same issues. It provided an opportunity for NGOs to network and lobby governments. The conference's chief concern was how to maintain the momentum of the positive steps already made and to avoid any backsliding in commitments made by governments in Beijing. Implementation was the largest concern and more funding is essential if targets are to be met. It was agreed that the goals set out in the Platform for Action had not been fully implemented, and further initiatives were needed. Delegates agreed that periodic reviews can jumpstart governments into action. Women Parliamentarians and women's organizations must continue to apply external and internal pressure on governments if implementation is to be accelerated.

The conference closed with general agreement among the fifty-six participants that the universal goal of economic development is inexorably tied to the social, political and economic empowerment of women, and that this will only be achieved by the joint efforts of the women and men of the world.

19 What works and what does not for women in politics: a Commonwealth perspective

Extracts from a presentation by the Commonwealth Parliamentary Association (CPA) to the Sixth Commonwealth Meeting of Ministers Responsible for Women Affairs, New Delhi, India, April 2000

Affirmative Action

Although a woman's right to vote and run for elected office is legally established, at the present time only one of the fifty-four member nations of the Commonwealth can boast that it has 30 per cent or more women in its national Parliament though some Commonwealth countries have achieved or topped that figure in the past.[1] For example, in June 1993 female membership of the Seychelles Parliament stood at 45.8 per cent.

One successful method used by several Commonwealth countries to guarantee a minimum number of women in their national legislatures is by the use of quotas, either by reserving seats in Parliament and other public offices by law, or by political parties targeting candidates.

Fifteen of the 225 parliamentary seats in Tanzania are reserved for women (in total there are 46 women Members), as are 30 of Bangladesh's 330 seats (the women are elected by the 300 elected MPs). The 1995 Ugandan Constitution specifies that the Parliament will have one woman representative for every district (there are fifty-one women MPs in the Parliament).

In India, the seventy-third and seventy-fourth constitutional amendments of 1993 reserved 30 per cent of Panchayat seats for women, as a means of fostering women's greater political participation, and in 1998 new attempts to extend the same reservation to seats in the state legislatures and national Parliament were initiated, though have not to date been successful.

In several jurisdictions, the initiative to take positive action to ensure women's participation in Parliament has been taken by political parties, which have developed their own regulations to ensure that a certain number of women are represented in executive positions within the party, and are adopted as electoral candidates.

Canada's New Democratic Party was the first party in North America to guarantee gender parity on its executives and on all of its governing bodies and committees. The Victoria (Australia) Labor Party has constitutionally guaranteed since 1945 (when the party was formed) that 50 per cent of office bearers should be women.[2] There are parties in the United Kingdom, Zimbabwe and Zambia that have women's wings with mandatory representation at national level.

The British Labour Party employed all-women shortlists in selecting some of its candidates in the run-up to the 1997 election, and despite a legal challenge which forced its subsequent early abandonment, large numbers of Labour women entered Parliament (the Labour Party won 101 of the 119 seats won by women).[3] The Labour Party now has a target of 40 per cent of party seats being filled by women.

The Australian Labor Party adopted a 25 per cent target for women candidates after the 1980 elections, which resulted in a steady increase in the number of women elected to state and federal parliaments in the 1980s. In 1994, the Labor Party initiated affirmative action for women in the form of a 35 per cent quota in the pre-selection of candidates, the intention being:

> To produce an outcome where 35 per cent of public office positions held by Labour or a majority of seats needed to form government, whichever is the greater, will be filled by women … by the year 2002.[4]

Party measures such as the above work, especially if women candidates, equally with men, are placed in constituencies where the party is likely to win. Running female candidates exclusively in marginal seats (or seats the party has no chance of winning) is mere lip-service.

Women candidates apparently hold significant electoral appeal for voters. In Australia in the 1990 elections, surveys revealed that women were between 2 and 3 per cent more likely to vote for a woman candidate, while men's attitudes were split fifty–fifty. In the 1992 elections in the United Kingdom, women candidates were found to have a clear 1 per cent advantage, crucial in marginal seats.[5] Few parties across the Commonwealth seem to have taken this on board – that women candidates win.

According to the Inter-Parliamentary Union (IPU), quotas established by political parties are more successful than those set by law, but very few parties have adopted such policies.

The use of quotas to ensure representation for women provokes strong reactions. Those in favour of quotas, reserved seats and other affirmative action measures argue that if the system militates against women securing nomination and election in their own right, then new systems should be devised to 'level the playing field'. Proponents argue that a female perspective is required in Parliament, that men cannot adequately represent women, and that women's equal representation in Parliament is a right which is not being upheld. Some form of affirmative action is therefore justified. Most feel that quotas should be a temporary 'pump-priming' mechanism, which will alter the perception of politics as an exclusively male preserve.

Opponents to affirmative action measures argue that they are undemocratic and unfair. They fear that women fast-streamed into Parliament by such schemes are likely to be less qualified and effective than Parliamentarians who got into the House on their own merit, and that such weak role models will be damaging to the perception of women MPs. The views of Ann Carlton, a senior Labour party figure, on the aborted British Labour Party quota system are typical:

> The policy is designed to increase the number of women in Parliament. I am in favour of that aim, but I deeply resent the

> method. Are we the 'little women' to be spoken down to and condescendingly given a helping hand? To treat women in this way is patronizing. It is unpopular. It is manifestly unfair. Add the words undemocratic and foolish, and you have the new quota system in a nutshell.[6]

Ideally quotas should be used as a temporary, interim measure, as a means of kick-starting a change in the political landscape. They cannot be a long-term solution.

Appointed/Nominated Seats

In many bicameral Commonwealth parliaments, upper house membership is filled by appointment, with typically the selection being proportionately made by the Head of Government, Leader of the Opposition and Governor-General.[7] This presents a unique opportunity for party leaders to ensure that women are represented in Parliament, particularly if very few women were elected to the lower house. The Trinidadian Senate has a 32 per cent female membership, whilst the House of Representatives has 11 per cent; the Jamaican Senate is 24 per cent female, but its House of Representatives has 13 per cent women, while the 11 per cent female membership of the Barbados House of Assembly is more than tripled in the Senate, where 33 per cent of the membership is female. In Canada, the appointed Senate is 29 per cent female, whilst women constitute 20 per cent of the elected lower house.

An examination of the CPA's Women in Parliament database reveals that in one case at least (Bermuda), women who were formerly Senate appointees are now elected Members of the lower house (at least two of the seven women Members have this experience).[8] This suggests that service as an appointed Senator can act as a springboard for women to run for election in the lower house. Possible reasons might be increased confidence as a result of parliamentary and political experience gained in the Senate, the opportunity to develop better networks, and being able to develop a higher positive public profile thereby becoming more 'electable'.

In Singapore, since the introduction of the Nominated Member of Parliament (NMP) provision (implemented from 1990) the number of women in the Parliament has increased, from four in 1990 (all elected) to six in 2000 (four elected, two NMPs, that is, the NMP provision has increased the number of women in Parliament by 50 per cent).[9]

Similarly, in legislatures where provision exists for a nominated Member to represent a specific population (for example, an Anglo-Indian representative is appointed in some Indian parliaments, and in the case of the state Legislative Assembly of West Bengal, a woman holds this office), appointing a woman to the post can be used to increase the overall number of women in Parliament.

Changing the Electoral System

The impact of the electoral system has long been identified as one of the factors impeding the progress of women in electoral politics.

Countries that have adopted a form of proportional representation (PR) consistently elect more women than countries with single-Member plurality systems or first past the post (FPTP) systems such as in Canada and the United Kingdom. Lisa Young, a Canadian student of politics, found from researching twenty-three democracies that 'the type of electoral system is the most significant predictor of the number of women elected'.[10] The proportion of women in Australia's upper houses is generally higher than in lower houses, and this is commonly considered to be as a result of the system of PR employed for upper house elections.[11]

Following the introduction of the MMP (mixed member proportional) electoral system in New Zealand in 1996, there was a 10 per cent increase in women's representation, though whether this was as a result of the new electoral system or part of a continuing trend toward greater political participation by women is unclear. After decades of research into women's political participation and the impact of the electoral system thereon, the IPU has concluded: 'it seems safe to state that the proportional system is the most conducive to the election of women … provided that a number of safeguards are applied'.[12] That said, regardless of what electoral system is in place, it seems obvious that in countries where representation in Parliament is driven and defined by political parties (which is the case in most of the sovereign countries of the Commonwealth), change in the form of increased numbers of women in Parliament will only occur if political parties are committed to bringing it about. In FPTP systems, political parties (with centralized candidate selection machinery) could choose 50 per cent female candidates in all 'winnable' and marginal seats. In PR systems, parties could alternate male and female candidates in their lists, every other list being headed by a woman. The electoral system therefore need not be a barrier to women entering politics if parties chose to adopt a different approach in their candidate selection.

Political parties by and large are unlikely to adopt such a method of operation without demands for change from society at large.

The May 1999 mixed PR/FPTP elections for the first Scottish Parliament since 1707 returned a 129-seat Parliament of 37.2 per cent women. Thirty female constituency Members of the Scottish Parliament (MSPs) were elected by FPTP (out of seventy-three, that is, 41.1 per cent) and eighteen female regional MSPs (out of fifty-six, that is, 32.1 per cent) were elected by PR.

In the run-up to the recent elections in Scotland, organizations such as Engender – an information, research and networking body for women in Scotland – ran consciousness-raising campaigns on the importance of women being elected to the new Scottish Parliament.[13]

The National Executive of the Labour Party approved the principle of twinning constituencies where the party believed it had an equal chance of winning.[14] Thus Labour Party members in the two constituencies cast two votes in the selection of candidates. The first vote was for a candidate on a list comprised only of women, and the second vote for a candidate from a list comprised only of men. The candidate polling the highest number of votes chose which of the two constituencies s/he wished to contest. The candidate who topped the other list contested the second constituency. Of fifty-six seats in total won by the Labour Party in Scotland, women won exactly 50 per cent.

The second largest party represented in the Parliament, the Scottish National Party, won thirty-five seats in total, of which fifteen (or 42.9 per cent) were won by women. This was achieved without any special mechanism to ensure women's representation.

The Scottish experience will doubtless be extensively studied over the coming months, in order to understand how the combination of factors outlined above (electoral system, party affirmative action, public attitudes and expectations) resulted in so many women being returned to Parliament.

This paper has attempted to provide a Commonwealth overview of 'what works' in getting women into Parliament. Whilst recognizing that 'what works' for one jurisdiction may not be feasible or appropriate in another, what is certain is that if the Commonwealth's agreed target of women occupying 30 per cent of decision-making places in the political, public and private sectors by the year 2005 is to become a reality rather than a vague ambition, then many Commonwealth countries over the next five years will have to make radical changes to bring that about.[15]

Notes

1 It should be noted however that several Chambers of Commonwealth Parliaments in 1999 do have 30 per cent or more women Members. The Australian Senate has a 31.6 per cent female membership; the Barbados Senate has 33.3 per cent; the Belize Senate has 44.4 per cent, while the Senate of Canada and the New Zealand House of Representatives are within 1 per cent or so of that figure. Further, several Commonwealth chambers of state, provincial or territorial legislatures have achieved the 30 per cent target. The new Parliament in Scotland comprises 37.2 per cent women Members.

2 Coopers and Lybrand, *Women and Parliaments in Australia and New Zealand: A Discussion Paper* for the Commonwealth-State Ministers Conference on the Status of Women (September 1994, p. 15).

3 For a discussion of the Labour Party's policy in Scotland, see below.

4 Margaret Reynolds, *The Last Bastion: Labor Women Working Towards Equality in the Parliaments of Australia,* Business and Professional Publishing, 1995, pp. 82 and 130.

5 Western Australia State Parliamentary Labor Party submission to the CPA Task Force formed to research 'Barriers to Women's Participation in Parliament', whose findings were published by the CPA in March 1996.

6 *Daily Mail*, 25 May 1995.

7 For example, the Senates of Barbados, Jamaica, St Lucia, Trinidad and Tobago.

8 This database comprises biographical data on all the women Parliamentarians in the 142 CPA parliaments, which include state, provincial and territorial legislatures across the Commonwealth.

9 In moving the second reading of the NMP Bill in 1989, then First Deputy Prime Minister Mr Goh Chok Tong gave three reasons for the introduction of the scheme: '(i) to allow for a greater airing of alternative views, (ii) to enable Singaporeans who would not otherwise enter politics to participate, and (iii) to increase the number of MPs from under-represented groups, such as women'. *The Parliamentarian*, April 1999, p. 25, Singapore supplement, Unelected Representatives article by Dr Lee Tsao Yuan, NMP.

10 Lisa Young, MA thesis in political science, *Women in National Legislatures: An Evaluation of the Strategy of Pursuing Power for Women Through the Legislative Route in Nordic and Anglo-American Democracies* (Carleton University, Ottawa), quoted in the Nunavut Implementation Commission's Press Release, December 6 1994.

11 Coopers and Lybrand, *Women and Parliaments in Australia and New Zealand*, p. 7.

12 IPU, *What Has Worked*, p. 9.

13 Engender's website can be found at http://www.engender.org.uk

14 The Labour Party, in conjunction with the Liberal Democratic Party, forms the first Scottish Government.

15 Past and present Members of the CWP Steering Committee have generously shared their experiences and perceptions with the author of this paper, but any errors, inaccuracies, omissions or personal views expressed are claimed as the author's own.

20 Institutional framework for mainstreaming gender in public service personnel management

Commonwealth Secretariat

The Commonwealth has developed the Gender Management System (GMS) as a means of mainstreaming gender throughout national governments. The GMS is defined as a set of structures, mechanisms and processes to ensure that gender considerations are integrated into all government policies, programmes and activities. The establishment and running of a GMS takes place within a particular political, economic, social and cultural context – the enabling environment of the GMS.

This chapter examines the enabling environment of the GMS, the GMS structures and mechanisms, and how they relate to the structures and functions of public service personnel management systems in many Commonwealth countries.

Gender mainstreaming is about bringing about organizational change, which requires concrete action. However, before such action can be carried out effectively, it is necessary to obtain a diagnosis of the particular gender problem in the country, its historical origins, how deeply rooted it is, and so on. This diagnostic process takes the form of gender analysis, which is examined in the following chapter, along with the GMS processes as applied to public service personnel management.

Enabling Environment

A programme of gender mainstreaming in the public service requires a positive enabling environment including political will at the highest level, legal and administrative frameworks that are conducive to gender equality, and sufficient resources for the programme's implementation. Where any of these elements is lacking, lobbying, advocacy and awareness raising are necessary on the part of the National Women's Machinery or Women's Bureau, as well as other interested parties, to bring about the requisite change in consciousness for a suitably enabling environment.

Public service commissions and central personnel agencies can, through their supervisory role of the whole administration system, play an important role in bringing about this change in consciousness by identifying targets, giving policy advice to stakeholders regarding gender mainstreaming, and securing implementation of gender-positive policies.

The Structures of a GMS

The interrelated structures of the GMS are designed to provide a strong and sustainable institutional framework for gender mainstreaming.

A central component of the GMS is the Gender Management Team, which consists of the Permanent Secretaries of core government ministries, such as Finance, Development Planning, Justice, Women's/Gender Affairs and the Public Service.

The Gender Management Team would also include at least one representative of civil society, such as the head of the National Commission on Gender Equality.

The role of the Gender Management Team is to provide leadership for the mainstreaming of gender in the core ministries and to establish broad operational policies, indicators to measure the effectiveness of those policies and timeframes for their implementation.

A GMS also includes other institutional arrangements for mainstreaming gender:

- Gender focal points: two or more designated senior staff members in each core and line ministry, whose role is to serve as in-house

gender experts, share information on gender issues and promote gender mainstreaming in their ministries.
- An Inter-Ministerial Steering Committee with representatives from core and line ministries; these would normally be the gender focal points in each ministry.
- A Commission or Council on gender equality.
- A Parliamentary Gender Caucus consisting of gender-aware Parliamentarians.

Public service commissions and central personnel agencies have a key role to play in setting up the various institutional structures of the Gender Management System. While the gender focal points will be nominated by their respective departments, public service commissions and/or central personnel agencies can work with the lead agency, that is, the national women's machinery (Women's Bureau or Ministry of Women's Affairs) to develop these institutional structures and ensure that nominations are forthcoming for the various positions.

The GMS structures function within the context of the particular organization or agency in which they are established. In the case of public service management systems, this context is undergoing change and varies according to particular national circumstances.

Structure and Functions of Public Service Management Systems

In many Commonwealth countries, public service commissions have been fashioned mainly after the British Civil Service Commission. For all but a few Commonwealth countries, provisions relating to public service commissions were written into the founding constitutions on achieving independence. In the subregion of East and Southern Africa, for example, the public service commissions all have the same thread running through them of their functions being spelt out succinctly in the constitution.

An important function of the public service commission is to uphold and protect the public service's traditional values, namely, neutrality, selection by merit, and probity and integrity. Each of these values has a particular gender dimension.

Neutrality

One of the aims in creating public service commissions in Commonwealth countries at the time of independence was to safeguard the political neutrality of the public service. For this reason, public services can be resistant to changes made by governments to their status and functioning (Polidano and Manning 1996: 7–9). So even when there is political will towards adopting more gender-aware practices and approaches, change may not come rapidly.

Selection by Merit

The merit principle is regarded as one of the foundation stones of the public service. However, it raises some important issues when looked at from a gender perspective. In many countries of the Commonwealth, educational and career opportunities have over several generations been far more available to men than to women. Although women are catching up with men in education and work experience in a number of countries, a narrow application of the merit principle, based only on the past training and experience of the applicant, could nevertheless result in a disproportionate number of jobs being awarded to male applicants.

Two approaches may be adopted to correct this imbalance without prejudicing the merit principle: positive action and affirmative action.

Positive action means taking special steps to encourage people from under-represented groups (for example, women) to apply for a post, and to ensure that the recruitment and selection process is welcoming to them. However, at the point of selection, all candidates are treated equally. This means that there is no preference given to any group.

Affirmative action means that the interview board selects a candidate from an under-represented group (for instance, a woman) where he or she is suitably qualified for the position (based on criteria set by the board), in preference to any other candidate who also meets the requirements.

Only if the selected candidate is less well qualified than another can it be argued that the merit principle is being breached.

However, merit is a function not only of the past experience of the applicant but also of the stated requirements of any specified job. The inclusion in the job specifications of a requirement that the incumbent be aware of and experienced in dealing with gender issues would serve to increase the numbers of decision-makers who are gender-sensitive and can take gender-informed decisions.

Probity and Integrity

These traditional values of the public service can be brought to bear on gender mainstreaming through the understanding that women's rights are human rights, and that the denial of equality for women is a breach of their human rights. Probity and integrity require a respect for human rights.

Most public service commissions work in collaboration with a government ministry, variously referred to as the Ministry of the Public Service or Central Personnel Office. The Central Personnel Office is part of the executive and fully accountable to the Government. It deals with matters not under the remit of the public service commission, which can include job creation and classification, staff training and development, and determining pay and conditions of work (Polidano and Manning 1996: 11).

Increasingly, a third set of players in public service personnel management is made up of line ministries and departments, to whom some decisions relating to staff appointments, promotions, training and discipline are delegated.

There are therefore three strategic points of entry for gender mainstreaming in the management of public service personnel: the public service commission itself, the Central Personnel Office, and the line departments.

Between them, these three players are responsible for three major areas of personnel management:

- appointments and promotions (of both senior and junior/middle grades) and setting terms and conditions of employment
- discipline and
- staff training.

21 Affirmative action in the Commonwealth Secretariat

Commonwealth Secretariat

The 1995 Commonwealth Plan of Action on Gender and Development introduces a vision in which 'the Commonwealth works towards a world in which women and men have equal rights and opportunities at all stages of their lives'. This vision reflects the 1991 Harare Commonwealth Declaration which includes in the Commonwealth's Fundamental Principles:

> Equal rights for all citizens regardless of gender, race, colour, creed or political belief (and) equality for women, so that they may exercise their full and equal rights.

The Commonwealth Secretariat, under its commitment to support the implementation of the Plan of Action and serve as a model of good employment practice, agreed to work to a target of 33 per

Table 21.1 Secretariat staff: comparative figures (%)

Year	*Deputy Secretary General*	*Female Directors*	*Female Special Adviser/Deputy Directors*	*Female professional staff*	*Female support staff*
1995	0	7.1	22.5	29.3	76.6
1997	0	14.3	27.0	31.5	76.8
1999	33.3	14.3	25.3	34.1	75.9
2000	33.3	23.0	31.25	34.4	76.31

cent of women in senior grades by 2000. To achieve this target, the organization further committed to adopt exceptional measures, including affirmative action to 'attain gender and geographical balance in the composition of the staff'. This was formally incorporated into the Commonwealth Secretariat's *Equal Employment Opportunities Policy (EEOP)* in 1997.

PART 2

Preface to chapters 22 and 23

Without doubt, more and more countries and parliaments are appreciating that women have a right to participate in political structures and legislative decision-making. However, for the most part, although women may overcome the more general obstacles to their participation in parliaments, once they reach there they often encounter additional difficulties.

In 1998 the Commonwealth Parliamentary Association (CPA) collaborated with three Commonwealth legal NGOs in the development of the Latimer House Guidelines on Parliamentary Supremacy and Judicial Independence. Among many other matters, the guidelines point out the need to improve the numbers of women Members in Commonwealth parliaments, and suggest ways in which this goal can be achieved. An earlier CPA study had already identified barriers to the participation of women in public life. The next logical step was to endeavour to identify means by which the task facing women Parliamentarians can be rationalized.

Against this background, in February and March 2001 the CPA, with the assistance of the CPA Malaysia Branch and the approval of the CPA Executive Committee, arranged a Study Group in Kuala Lumpur, Malaysia, on 'Gender-sensitizing Commonwealth parliaments'. The aims of the Study Group were set out as:

- To share analyses, experiences and good practices of Standing Orders in Commonwealth parliaments.
- To identify concrete strategies and mechanisms to make Commonwealth parliaments as gender-sensitive as possible.
- To prioritize key areas for action, based on the recommendations of the Study Group.

This Study Group was set up in furtherance of a suggestion made originally by the Steering Committee of the Commonwealth Women Parliamentarians (CWP) that it was necessary to examine conventions and language embedded in Standing Orders that possibly affect behaviour and attitudes towards women. The focus of this Study Group was, however, widened to include considerations of other aspects of parliamentary life that women find alienating or difficult.

Highly participatory and interactive discussions focused on the female Parliamentarian, and discussed the challenges and impediments she faces from the stage of standing for a seat in Parliament to her participation in the parliamentary process, after election.

I extend the thanks of the CPA to the Study Group Members and advisers, to the CPA Malaysia Branch for providing a congenial venue, and to my colleagues Raja Gomez and Anthony Staddon, respectively Director and Assistant Director of Development and Planning, for their valuable contribution to the organization and delivery of these successful deliberations.

The report in Chapter 22, prepared by Ms Jacqui Sampson-Jacent, Clerk of the House of Representatives of Trinidad and Tobago and Rapporteur to the Group, identifies the issues discussed by the Study Group and presents to the reader the Group's recommendations, which I hope will assist parliaments and their Members to understand better the difficulties faced by women Parliamentarians.

In particular, the report was presented to Commonwealth Parliamentarians and parliamentary officials attending the 47th Commonwealth Parliamentary Conference held in September 2001 in Canberra, Australia. Conference participants discussed the general subject of gender representation and many of the specific ideas developed by the Study Group. Summaries of their discussions are contained in the chapters following the report.

In a wider perspective, it is the Association's hope that the extensive commentary and recommendations for future action will inform many of the current debates in national and sub-national parliaments, both within and outside the Commonwealth, and have a substantial positive impact on the way in which parliaments conduct their business.

Arthur R. Donahoe, QC
Secretary-General
Commonwealth Parliamentary Association
1993–2001

22 Report of the CPA study group on gender-sensitizing Commonwealth parliaments

Ms Jacqui Sampson-Jacent

Introduction

When Nancy Astor, the first female Member of Parliament to take her seat in the UK House of Commons, entered Parliament for the first time, it is said that her male colleagues went out of their way to make the experience as difficult and embarrassing as possible. From being refused a seat on the corner of the back benches, requiring her to clamber over the legs of other Parliamentarians, to searching for the toilet in the most inaccessible part of the parliamentary estate, it must have been a sobering experience.[1]

Admittedly, since the days of Nancy Astor, there have been many changes in the environment of parliaments as well as in the participation of women in legislative work. The UK Parliament, for example, introduced in the autumn of 2000 more 'family friendly' sitting hours, with debates on bills ending at 2200 hours from Mondays to Wednesdays (MPs were already free to leave early on Thursdays). A less controversial initiative was opened for trial periods in 2000 and 2001, namely a children's playgroup in the Palace of Westminster.

Women in the South African Parliament have been instrumental in creating an environment in which women are comfortable. Session times have been changed, a crèche has been established, and the rules governing attire have all been altered because of the influence of women Members.

It is also true that women Members across the Commonwealth have not only made a difference to the ambience and procedures of Parliament, but also affected the type of legislation promulgated.

The principle of equality between men and women is enshrined in the United Nations Charter, the Universal Declaration of Human Rights and other international treaties, including the Convention on the Elimination of All Forms of Discrimination against Women (CEDAW), to which 154 states are parties. In addition, the Beijing Declaration and Platform for Action reaffirmed this commitment. And yet in practice, genuine power sharing for women remains elusive and distant.

This report summarizes the issues discussed by the Study Group and puts forward wide-ranging recommendations which, if implemented, would improve the overall functioning of Commonwealth legislatures and in the final analysis benefit Commonwealth countries and their peoples as a whole.

Challenges on the Road to Parliament

From the onset, the group acknowledged that ultimately, gender equality is inseparable from the wider goal of development, since any society that excludes 50 per cent of its population from playing a meaningful role in decision-making in that society is undermining itself and inhibiting its growth and development.

Against that backdrop, the Study Group noted that female representation in Commonwealth parliaments is not impressive, with women making up only about 13.8 per cent of Membership.[2] Progress has been mixed and varies widely among regions (see Table 22.1). Today, women's representation in the Lok Sabha, India, is only 49 Members out of 550 or 8.9 per cent of the total membership. In Sri Lanka it is 4 per cent, in Cyprus 7 per cent and Nigeria 3.4 per cent. In Canada, women represent 20 per cent of the House of the Commons and 32 per cent of the Senate. In several Caribbean countries, the proportion of women appointed to the Senate is relatively high while the share of women elected to the lower Chamber by direct vote is low. For example, in Trinidad and Tobago, women represent 32 per cent of the membership of

Table 22.1 Female representation in Parliament by region

Region	*Percentage of women in Parliament (including national, state, federal and provincial parliaments)*
Africa	15.5
Asia	5.8
Australia	24.7
British Isles and the Mediterranean	18.6
Canada	22.2
Caribbean, the Americas and the Atlantic	17.5
Pacific	8.7
South East Asia	8.5

Source: www.cpahq.org

the appointed Senate but only 10 per cent of the elected House of Representatives.

There are many legislatures where the proportion of women may be small but they occupy a large percentage of high-ranking posts. Whether these legislatures offer better terms on which women Members may participate is a matter for debate.

Women's strongest representation is in northern Europe, particularly in the Nordic countries. For example, women hold 73 out of 200 seats (36.5 per cent) in the Finnish Parliament. In the term beginning in the spring of 1996, the Speaker and both Deputy Speakers of the Parliament were women. It is important to note that nineteen women were elected to the first unicameral Parliament of Finland in 1907.

In the Commonwealth, women's representation at the top levels of government is similarly disappointing. Women constitute a small percentage of cabinet ministers, with responsibility generally confined to areas such as social affairs, education, and health and family matters. While women are key contributors to economic development, they are almost completely absent from ministries of finance, trade and economic planning. And although women have suffered as victims of wars and other conflicts, they are rarely found in ministries of defence or foreign affairs, and their participation in preventive diplomacy or conflict resolution continues to be extremely limited. Women felt they would be strong additions to these portfolios.

It was acknowledged that in almost every society patriarchal values are constantly reinforced through traditions, religion, customs and socio-political structures which are difficult to change and that, generally, there is very little effort to encourage women to take on positions of public responsibility. There was support for the view that in reality women are discouraged against giving up 'their domestic responsibilities' in order to enter the world of politics. The Study Group therefore concluded that more effort is needed to encourage women to enter politics and Parliament, and concerted efforts should be made to eliminate systemic barriers especially in the party process to nomination in winnable constituencies.

It was felt that regular programmes of youth training and empowerment, such as local, regional and international youth parliamentary debates, should be undertaken to encourage young women to get involved in politics. The Group commended the CPA for its role in such efforts, and stressed the need for the CPA to continue to sponsor and support local, regional and international Youth Parliaments. Other activities recommended are essay-writing competitions at all levels, and institutionalized training activities that the Group believed should also be encouraged within the political party.

In addition, the Study Group maintained that experienced female Parliamentarians should play a vibrant role in encouraging young women to enter politics. It was suggested that they should visit schools, universities and other institutions to give lectures that could include accounts of their experiences. They should also invite young female politicians to accompany them at meetings and other public gatherings, as this will help eradicate the perception that older politicians feel threatened by younger colleagues.

The Study Group felt that state funding, insofar as it is economically feasible, is necessary in order to encourage women and young persons to participate in elections. The suggestion that specific party funding should be provided to encourage women to run for seats in Parliament was also strongly supported. Parties should encourage male and female delegate selection to all their conventions.

There was consensus therefore that changing attitudes towards political participation of women, and sensitizing the political system to accept women, require a co-coordinated effort at various levels, by governments, parliaments and other decision-making bodies, political parties, civil society including academic institutions, the media and inter-governmental organizations, as well as the family unit. There was overwhelming support for the view that, in the final analysis, political participation of women cannot be achieved without certain underlying concerns being addressed, including:

- Women themselves have to be made aware of their political rights in, and political obligations to, society.
- Men have to be sensitized to the unconscionable nature of gender inequity in politics.
- The political party must recognize the need to provide support for women candidates.
- Political commitment to gender equity has to be established firmly at national and international levels.
- Legal actions have to flow from this political commitment.
- The legal regime has to reflect this commitment in letter and spirit.

The Study Group agreed that the concern related to women in politics is not only about the number of them who succeed in running for parliamentary office but the ways in which they can be effective in Parliament. In pursuance of its main objective, the Study Group gave much attention to the major obstacles women face when entering Parliament and the means by which such obstacles could be overcome.

Removing the Obstacles

The Study Group believed that, once elected or appointed to Parliament, the female MP encounters additional barriers and limitations to her equal participation in political decision-making. Such obstacles were identified as follows:

Political

- The historical domination of politics and the political environment by the male gender.
- The prevalence of male political networks (both formal and informal).
- The traditional political power structure and its inbuilt bias against women.

Cultural and Economic

- The perception of women's subordination to male control and the necessity of male 'permission' to participate in public life.
- Lack of support from the family (emotional and sharing of domestic responsibilities) and the burden of having to successfully manage her domestic responsibilities and her professional obligations.
- Lack of adequate financial support.

Institutional Structures, Arrangements and Styles

- Inadequate training/orientation for women entering Parliament, on procedures, regulations and other technical information.
- Relative lack of women role models in Parliament.
- Hours of sittings.
- Seating and other physical arrangements within Parliament.
- Traditions, styles and norms of parliamentary debate and language.

Psychological

- The predetermined and psychologically established social roles that are assigned to men and women.
- The mass media and its attitude towards female Parliamentarians.

Removing the Political Obstacles

Without a doubt, parliaments are products of political processes that were male-dominated or exclusively male. Indeed, most established parliaments were created and organized by men, and have traditionally been reserved for them. Over the centuries males have established procedures at their own discretion. Even newly established legislatures, patterned after their predecessors, prove to be male dominated and reflect male influences and language. Consequently, upon entering Parliament, the female MP immediately realizes that she has entered a male domain.

The Study Group believed that through training and supporting women candidates and female Members of Parliament, entrants to Parliament could be prepared properly for their new role. It was agreed that such training should be undertaken by parliaments themselves as well as by political parties. Training by political parties would help incoming female MPs to understand more fully what is expected by their party and will help them understand their party's position on the legislative procedures and systems used in Parliament. Although in some parts of the Commonwealth political parties offer such training and orientation, the Group recognized that in many countries most parties do not have the resources and, more often than not, the willingness to offer such training. Women's commissions were utilized by some parties (for example, the Liberal Party in Canada) to do some of this training.

Support for the view that the political parties themselves should primarily be responsible for grooming new Members and initiating them also came from India, where many women move from the state assemblies to the Union Parliament. It was noted that in New Zealand there is a 'buddy' system in which every new Member has a 'buddy' who is an older Member. Within one party in New Zealand, ministers invite new Members to join them at meetings to familiarize the new recruits with their responsibilities and to parliamentary life. The Group also considered other ways in which New Zealand has managed to gain ground for women in politics and high office. It was postulated that the introduction of a system of proportional representation in New Zealand was a major contribution to a greater number of women in Parliament and new ways of working in Parliament.

The Group also concluded that female Parliamentarians could be assisted by a mechanism of networks both inter-party and intra-party, for the benefit of the female Member. It was accepted, though, that working at an inter-party level could be difficult as there are always tensions and a degree of mistrust. Indeed, not all women's issues achieve the degree of unanimity that they require and there are widening gaps on what were once agreed social platforms on policy for women and children. However, the Group suggested that areas of inter-party communication could be improved through internationally focused organizations, such as the CPA, and advocating greater equality of representation of women in Commonwealth parliaments. In this context, the Group maintained that the CPA's women's caucus, the Commonwealth Women Parliamentarians, must be appropriately funded and have representation on the Executive Committee of the CPA.

It was noted with commendation that the Minister of Women's Affairs in New Zealand calls a Joint Meeting of all female Members of Parliament at least once a month each parliamentary session, with emphasis being placed on policy rather than mutual party support. At the intra-party level, the New Zealand Labour Party has a Women's Council and a Women's Parliamentary Caucus. The party has a paid Women's Coordinator who attends Women's Caucus meetings and liaises with the party's Women's Council. All female Members of Parliament are invited and expected to take part in the Women's Council meetings when their schedules permit. The most important functions of the caucus are policy formulation and monitoring its implementation. It meets weekly when Parliament is sitting, and discusses and monitors legislation currently before the House that has a particular impact on women. The caucus, when appropriate, speaks as one voice when reporting back to the main party caucus. In addition, support at this level is available to female party Members through simple gestures like sitting besides a colleague when she is speaking in debate and the 'buddy' system where all new Members are paired with a senior Member primarily for their guidance.

In Canada, the Chair of the governing party's women's caucus reports to the prime minister in front of the entire party caucus each week the Parliament is sitting. The women's caucus invites ministers to talk to it on a regular basis, and asks questions of them about how the caucus can help them. The status of the female MP is further enhanced in this particular party by the rule that there must be male and female co-chairing at all party conventions. This helps women gain experience in presiding and handling major responsibilities, and increases public awareness of the strengths of women. It was also noted that in the Canadian Parliament, there is usually a woman deputy speaker and there is at least one woman on every parliamentary committee.

In India, there is a Women's Empowerment Parliamentary Committee. Its inter-party mandate is to consider how legislation impacts on women. However, it was noted that unfortunately (to date) this Standing Committee of Parliament has not been very successful in meeting its objectives.

It was therefore fully agreed that political parties, wherever they exist, have a role to play. It was felt that women's caucuses should be established; they must be active and vocal; and they should demand important parliamentary positions for women as well as key places within the government.

During the discussions on the role of the political party, there was a concern that the party should from time to time review the criteria for the exercise of a conscience vote on issues related to gender. This view held that the party should declare its position on such issues and require positive and supportive action by all its MPs, regardless of gender. Some participants felt that the criteria for deciding a conscience vote should be re-examined by political parties in Commonwealth parliaments, especially when the vote impacts on gender issues. However, it was recognized that differences in party structures between parliaments would have an impact on the universal application of this suggestion.

The Study Group also concluded that, regardless of the party's perspective on training and orientation for female MPs and on co-operation among women in Parliament, women MPs should inform themselves about gender issues and perspectives as they relate to their functioning in Parliament. Female MPs could achieve this by maintaining close links with women's organizations, particularly within their communities, to tap their knowledge and experiences and to be familiar with their concerns pertaining to the role of women in decision-making bodies. The Group felt that such liaisons also enhanced the legitimacy of the female MP while strengthening female political networks that were essential to sustain women who, despite the odds, strive for seats within their parliaments.

Removing the Cultural Obstacles

The Study Group agreed that cultural changes are necessary if Commonwealth parliaments are to become gender-sensitive. Any cultural changes must be profound and include efforts aimed at increasing gender awareness. Such efforts should also embrace changes to parliamentary procedures and methods of functioning geared towards accommodating the female MP.

> All Parliamentarians, not only those involved in policy development and analysis, should have an understanding of gender issues and be more gender-sensitive.

The Group maintained that to discharge their responsibilities properly, all Parliamentarians, and not only those involved in policy development and analysis, should have an understanding of gender issues and be more gender-sensitive. This understanding will only be achieved through training combined with specifically designed initiatives. In this regard, the Group suggested that all Commonwealth parliaments should be urged to commit to gender-based analyses of all parliamentary documents, including policy proposals, legislation and committee reports, in order to assess their impact on women and men, and to ensure that government policies, programmes and legislation are equitable for both sexes.

Gender-based analysis is defined as a process that assesses the differential impact of proposed and/or existing policies, programmes and legislation on men and women. It makes it possible for policy to be undertaken with an appreciation of gender differences, of the nature of relationships between women and men and of their different social realities, life expectation and economic circumstances. It is a tool for understanding social processes and for responding with informed and equitable options and compares how and why policy issues affect women and men. Gender-based analysis challenges the assumption that policies, programmes and legislation affect everyone in the same way regardless of gender.[3]

The Study Group was therefore pleased to hear of those parliaments, such as in Canada and Finland, where a committee has been established to consider and report on legislation with gender equity issues. In Canada, the procedural rules are often used by both men and women to influence the parliamentary agenda by introducing women's concerns into otherwise gender-blind debates, highlighting the fact that the life experiences of both sexes are different and that equity in numbers does not necessarily mean equal rights. Such tactics ensure that policies and legislation, once implemented, are equitable as far as possible for both men and women.

The consensus was that such positive actions combined with gender-sensitivity training would help eradicate the cultural barriers that impede the work of the female MP as well as remove the male's perception of a *female threat*. The Group therefore further recommended that women should be encouraged to network with their male counterparts and, if possible, work in association with them to break through established 'codes of conduct'. If this were done, male MPs would become increasingly more sensitized to gender issues. They would also appreciate that enabling female MPs to be effective representatives and legislators has important implications, not only politically, but also for the social and economic sectors of their communities.

There was full support for the suggestion that the CPA should sponsor an annual seminar with equal representation by male and female Members of Parliament, representative of the various branches of the Commonwealth, with the major objective of promoting gender-sensitivity, equality and inclusion. All delegations should have Members of both sexes included.

The Group maintained that Commonwealth parliaments should be encouraged to enact legislation to make changes that will benefit Commonwealth countries and their peoples. With this in mind, the Study Group endorsed the suggestion that, as far as possible, women and men in Parliament should be encouraged to propose laws for the improvement of the status of women and other marginalized social groups, and initiate new policy proposals favourable to women as well as to the wider society.

In order to reverse those traditional cultural barriers that work against women MPs, it was also suggested that Commonwealth governments should be urged to enact legislation with a clear declaration that the rights and obligations of men and women are identical. Such legislation should stipulate minimum quotas for women on decision-making bodies or, alternatively, introduce systems of affirmative action for representation by women in all areas of public life. Some countries already have this in their human rights legislation while others have statutes but little in the manner of real change.

During its discussions on cultural barriers, the Study Group found that, generally, the timing of parliamentary sessions does not take into consideration the many domestic duties faced by women. It was noted that, in many cases, the female Parliamentarian faces the burden of expectations from her own family and is assumed to be a super-human being: she must carry out her parliamentary responsibilities with breadth, depth and vigour; she is expected to be a better representative than her male counterpart; she must take care of her family, seeing to the care, protection and education of her children; she must ensure that the home is appropriate for her status in the society and certainly for that of her spouse; she must see to the well-being of her spouse, and she must, in the eyes of many, at all times be perfectly groomed. These are very high, if not impossible standards to be met at all times, and they are often standards not expected of their male colleagues.

Although concerns related to family responsibilities also relate to men, in most societies, despite widely changing attitudes, it is still considered that the mother is primarily responsible for the care of the family. Therefore lack of maternity benefits, day care facilities for children and separate rest rooms for women in Parliament restrict the participation of women in the political arena. Some countries have made physical accommodation with appropriate rest rooms, changing rooms and day care facilities.

'Democracy can only be achieved if the same opportunities are available to all. It is our responsibility to safeguard the future and put in place for the next generation of politicians, conditions that will allow them to serve.

Hon. Hazel Hannan, MKH, Isle of Man

It was the accepted view that across the Commonwealth, many women with young children have traditionally been deterred from entering politics for a number of reasons, including the lack of childcare facilities. In South Australia, for example, comparatively few women Members of Parliament have children of school age or less. Of the sixteen women Members in mid-1995, twelve had no children or their children had grown up and had left school. However, of the fifty-five men, twenty-six of them had children of school age.

The Study Group noted that the average age of women Parliamentarians in Finland is 42, which means that many of them are of childbearing age or have young families. In common with all other mothers in that country, a female Parliamentarian can take a maximum of 263 weekdays' maternity leave whereas a male Member is entitled to three weeks' paternity leave, all with full pay.

There was general agreement that all Commonwealth parliaments should be encouraged to consider introducing maternity and paternity benefits for Parliamentarians as well as citizens, and that proper facilities for the care of infants and young children should be established in Parliament buildings.

There was also concern that in many parliaments there is a high rate of divorce of persons elected to Parliament within the first two years of their being elected. The Group believed that where geographical factors require MPs, both male and female, to reside away from home, parliaments should, wherever possible, be encouraged to increase the level of travel, including air travel, permitted to MPs from their constituency to and from the capital as well as within the country generally. Such facilities should be extended to immediate family members.

The Group recommended that in those countries where, because of size and distance, it is necessary for MPs to utilize temporary accommodation nearer to Parliament, the parliamentary week should be narrowed with sittings for longer hours if required. This will free up more time for MPs to attend to constituency matters and to return home regularly.

The Group further recommended that, where applicable, Constituency Weeks should be free of committee work, removing the requirement for MPs to travel away from their constituencies or home territories during such weeks. Where possible they should coincide with school holidays.

It was also the consensus that Commonwealth parliaments should be urged to be more flexible in the amount of time off allowed for family purposes for Parliamentarians and that, where possible, the good convention of pairing should be introduced for dealing with necessary absences by MPs.

Removing the Institutional Obstacles

The Study Group spent a considerable amount of time considering the measures to alter the institution of Parliament to make it as gender-sensitive as possible.

> In addition to programmes especially geared for women, Parliament-sponsored training and orientation programmes involving both men and women are essential.

It was accepted that for women to be effective Parliamentarians, they must clearly understand the role and functions of the legislature and they must learn the rules by which it operates, both written and unwritten. All agreed that women must first learn the internal practices of their respective Parliament in order to equip themselves to utilize these rules to advance women's interests and goals.

A new female MP can acquire knowledge of parliamentary rules and practices in a variety of ways, including specific training and orientation programmes as well as more general socialization processes.

In the South Australian House of Assembly, introductory training is provided to all new Members following every election. In addition, Legislative Council staff also carry out less formal induction exercises for new Members that have been found to be more effective. This training includes information and instruction in many areas, including daily proceedings; Chamber procedures; rules of debate; facilities and legislation applicable to Members; parliamentary privilege and the committee system.

However, throughout most of the Commonwealth no specific structured training for female Parliamentarians exists. It was believed that this lack of training is a great impediment to women entering Parliament and delays their optimal participation in the parliamentary process. The Group therefore believes that special training for the female MP is essential if she is to overcome the many barriers to her successfully taking her seat in Parliament.

Nevertheless, in addition to programmes especially geared for women, training and orientation programmes involving both men and women are also important. It was stressed that such programmes should be sponsored by parliaments and should be held on a regular basis throughout each parliamentary session, particularly in the larger parliaments. The Group agreed that areas of training should include the following:

- all aspects of parliamentary practice and procedure
- computer training, including PowerPoint for the making of presentations
- time management
- speed-reading
- voice projection
- dealing with difficult people
- media training
- gender-sensitivity and equity training
- language training
- public speaking
- the process of law making
- the parliamentary library and its facilities.

As already mentioned, the Study Group noted that in every aspect, Parliament as an institution was designed to be, and has always been, the preserve of the male sex. It therefore follows that even at the level of language and communication, the institution is considered to be male-oriented. For example, 'he' includes 'she', and other formal and informal parliamentary language is used to let women know that Parliament is a male preserve.

Terms like 'manning' and 'manpower' persist instead of 'staff' and 'personnel'. So do 'man in the street' instead of 'person in the street', 'one-man one-vote' instead of 'one-person one-vote' and 'chairman' instead of 'chairperson' or 'chair'. Terms of endearment such as 'luv', 'm'dear' and 'sweetheart' are sometimes used and, consciously or not, belittle women in an incredibly male-chauvinistic arena. Women Parliamentarians do not find this endearing or amusing, and at best they tolerate these unacceptable practices.

There was a view that in many cases women who have been elected become complacent or are intimidated. Many women tend not to like non-sexist terms like 'chair' instead of 'chairman', or they continue to use terms such as 'manning' instead of 'staffing' because they perceive this attitude as being feminist and something with which they do not wish to be aligned. On the other hand, if a female Member takes a stand she is accused of being strident, overbearing or plain ridiculous, and even women join in the mockery.

It is the recommendation of the Group that Standing Orders should be amended to reflect gender-neutral language. Moreover, it is further recommended that gender-inclusive language should be a requirement in all public institutions and forums, and that early gender-sensitizing education of boys and girls should be pursued.

> Standing Orders should be amended to reflect gender-neutral language and, wherever possible, seating arrangements should be instituted to foster a less combative atmosphere more amenable to constructive debate.

The Study Group is of the view that the Westminster-style debating chamber is a competitive forum designed for men and reflecting male values. There was consensus that adversarial parliaments naturally encourage theatrical posturing and aggressive behaviour that often degenerates to the personal, which many women (and some men) find uncomfortable. The Group was disturbed to learn that in some jurisdictions undignified comments with sexual undertones, directed at women, have been allowed. Such an atmosphere is disrespectful and is likely to discourage women's participation. Here, the Speaker must also be vigilant.

The Study Group recommended that, wherever possible, seating arrangements should be instituted to foster a less combative atmosphere more amenable to constructive debate. There was also consensus that Speakers should encourage a high standard of debate, and that provisions in Standing Orders against the use of offensive and insulting language should be strictly observed.

Moreover, it was felt that female Parliamentarians should be encouraged to raise Points of Order more regularly, whenever such orders are breached.

The Study Group noted that generally there is an absence of a dress code for women in most parliaments. It was recognized that in many legislatures although women were expected to follow in the footsteps of men, hence the Westminster-style 'dark suits', issues related to dress posed no real difficulties for the female Member. Still, most agreed that the psychology of dress is the real issue, and that women need to remember that the professional judgement of their constituents is important.

Many felt that the expectation, perhaps self-imposed, that women would wear a variety of clothing, places an expense on women that does not exist, to the same extent, for men. Moreover, the media and the public generally focus unnecessarily on women's attire and not sufficiently on the policy issues that the female MP may be dealing with.

It was noted with concern that in some parliaments there still exist rules pertaining to dress that could be construed as discriminating against women. For example in the South Australia House of Assembly, Standing Order 131, which states that: 'Every Member desiring to speak shall rise from his seat on the benches, uncovered [hat removed], and address himself to the Speaker', has been held to include a woman who chooses to wear a hat in Parliament. The Study Group believed that any Standing Orders that relate primarily to an earlier era should be amended or deleted entirely, wherever they still exist.

The Study Group agreed with the view that institutional customs as well as rules, to a lesser degree, determine who gets important legislative positions and opportunities such as prime speaking times on the floor of the House. The Group noted that customs vary from country to country; but generally factors like party position, seniority, knowledge and expertise and popularity were the main contributors.

With this in mind, the Study Group suggested that women within legislatures should identify key positions and opportunities in Parliament and devise ways and avenues to get women into these positions. All agreed that the appointment of women to key parliamentary positions is an encouragement to women generally and provides opportunities for female MPs to make an impact and advance their careers. The Study Group was therefore pleased to learn that women are represented on all of the fourteen Special Committees in the Finnish Parliament and that women chair six of them.

It was observed that women appointed to government are usually assigned less prominent portfolios such as health, education and community affairs. The Study Group believed it is necessary to establish women's presence in the more prestigious and traditionally influential positions within parliaments and governments, for example finance and foreign affairs, although it was accepted that those areas customarily assigned to women are of national importance as well.

The Study Group believed that efforts to ensure that women are appointed to serve on, as well as chair, important committees and to prominent government offices could, wherever necessary, include amendments to standing orders and legislation. Moreover, it was agreed that standing orders should be reviewed regularly and, whenever necessary, amended, to ensure that the presence of women and issues pertaining to gender are taken into account by parliaments. Pertinent reference was made to the Equality Between Men and Women Act, passed by the Finnish Parliament in 1986, which seeks to prevent direct and indirect discrimination based on gender. The Office of the Ombudsman for Equality monitors the observance of the Act. The Group believed that Commonwealth countries should, at the very least, have Ministries of Gender and Equality Affairs for the monitoring of issues related to women. In Canada the Secretary of State for Women's Issues participates in cabinet committees.

> Efforts to ensure that women are appointed to serve on, as well as chair, important committees and to prominent government offices could, if necessary, include amendments to standing orders and legislation.

Other suggested efforts geared towards ensuring that women are represented in high profile offices included fostering support from non-government women's organizations and the media as well as international pressure. It is also recommended that, since parliamentary rules evolve on the basis of practice, female MPs should be consistent in nominating and voting for women to the chairs of important committees and in proposing the names of their female colleagues for less formal positions in Parliament. It was also suggested that there should be established, primarily within the larger parliaments, a mechanism for monitoring all legislative appointments and for the drawing of attention to the absence or relative absence of women in key positions or committees.

In the area of information and databases, the Study Group recommended that all Members should be provided with computers and related equipment and with Internet access. Where this is not possible, they should have easy access to such facilities. Apart from the obvious benefits that this would bring, the Member will be able to keep abreast of the data collected by various groups and NGOs such as the Beijing Declaration, IPU Statistics, UN Reports and CPA Newsletters. Frequent publishing of gender statistics of all public and state enterprises should be done to keep Parliamentarians up to date and promote vigilance and responsiveness on gender equality issues.

The Study Group noted that co-operation among women in the Finnish Parliament is extremely high. Such co-operation is well organized through the existence of a network called the 'Network of Women in Finland's Parliament'. This Network brings together female Deputies across party lines to discuss issues of particular interest to women with the following key objectives:

- to promote equality between men and women
- to further the implementation of women's rights and
- to introduce the perspectives of women into the drafting of legislation.

This Network has to date been extremely successful. It meets with all groups and stakeholders within the society, arranges seminars and visits, takes part in international activity and co-operates with women Parliamentarians from other countries. It also meets with female students and has held parliamentary seminars for female students. Once each month, the Network holds what is called an 'information lunch' for all female Members and often invites Ministers to these lunches to raise issues and questions of importance to women that fall within the portfolio of the ministers invited.

The Study Group considered this model to be quite instructive, and took particular note of the fact that legislation introduced in the name of the Chair of the Network has been passed in the Finnish Parliament, with support being received from among all the parties and factions. The Network can only bring legislation forward if it relates to women, and all female Members must agree to its introduction. No controversial issues can be brought forward.

> When issues regarding women are raised in Parliament, women speak and debate, but it is very seldom that they unite for the common good especially if it goes against the party whip.
>
> Margaret Alva, MP, India

During this discussion, the Study Group agreed that cross-party networking could be a strategic tool for informally training women MPs and for familiarizing them with Parliament. It was held that female networks provide new recruits with knowledge held by long-standing MPs, acquired after many years in Parliament, and enables women MPs to come together to discuss their concerns and their potential for effectiveness.

The Group therefore recommended that female Parliamentarians should get together to discuss issues common to women. Toward this end, formal and informal women's networks should be set up within parliaments at an intra-party level and preferably at an inter-party level as well, and women should identify policy issues where cross-party co-operation can exist.

In addition, it is suggested that as an inter-party grouping, female Parliamentarians should work with the various groups in society, for example non-governmental women's organizations and (community) radio and television, to promote awareness by the population of gender and equality-sensitizing issues and create the environment for wider public support.

> The adage that a woman has to be twice as good to go half as far still holds true – which is why our leading women are so very, very good and such wonderful mentors and role models'.
>
> Dianne Yates, MP, New Zealand

The Study Group also found that mentoring by more experienced female MPs is another important way of socializing new women entrants and of providing special training to them. The New Zealand 'buddy' system was again commended, since it was found that that this system assisted newly elected Members to gain confidence. Against that backdrop, it was generally agreed that experienced women in politics should feel privileged to be utilized as role models to younger female Parliamentarians. The Group felt that new female Members must be assisted in every way possible by more experienced, longer-serving Members.

The Study Group maintained that to cope with the inbuilt barriers in parliaments and to secure equality women have had to adopt varying approaches. For example, the Group was of the firm view that women must maintain contact with their primary support base and hold regular debriefings with women in their political parties and constituencies. There was overwhelming agreement with the suggestion that women Parliamentarians must at all times ensure that women are part of the process of shaping the policies that emanate from Parliament. The Group agreed with the comment that where men can be dismissive or simply unaware, women as a group should stand firm on subjects related to their rights.

The Study Group also looked at ways in which women in politics have interacted with non-governmental organizations both locally and internationally, and commended those women who have successfully used coalitions and partnerships to strengthen their presence in Parliament.

In a related dimension, the Study Group suggested that communication links between women – within parliaments and between parliaments – should be maintained through newsletters, the Internet, publications and Websites.

The suggestion that all parliamentary delegations must include female representation was broadly accepted. The Group felt that Commonwealth parliaments and the CPA must be made aware of the fact that female Parliamentarians are anxious to be seen to be publicly doing their duties, not only locally but also internationally. It was noted that some parliaments continually send only token representations of women Parliamentarians.

There were lengthy discussions on the role that the CPA can play, particularly in regard to the representation by women on its Executive Committee. It was generally agreed that structural change is essential to move the process forward. The Study Group recognized that the attitude of the larger body reflected the attitude of the individual parliaments. It was agreed that women should represent at least 30 per cent of the Executive Committee by the year 2005 in line with the target that Commonwealth countries are working towards. The Group stressed that this should be brought to the urgent attention of all Branches and the Executive Committee of the CPA.

There were expressions of dissatisfaction over the fact that meetings of the Steering Committee of Commonwealth Women Parliamentarians are no longer funded and it was unanimously agreed to recommend to the CPA that funding for the CWP Steering Committee should be reintroduced. Moreover, the Group recommended that the CWP Meeting at the CPA annual Commonwealth Parliamentary Conference should be regarded as a regular plenary session attended by all delegates and that host branches should be advised to avoid conflict with other activities in the programme.

At the international level also, the Group believed that the CPA should regularly undertake an audit of its member states and parliaments, through the form of a questionnaire, with the objectives of assessing the extent to which Commonwealth governments fulfil their obligations with respect to the Beijing Declaration and CEDAW, and of judging the procedures and practices of parliaments from a gender perspective.

Removing the Psychological Barriers

The Study Group agreed with the view that one way to build women's parliamentary careers and promote their advancement into key positions is through the use of the media to increase the visibility and confidence of women Parliamentarians. However, it noted that the media is not generally kind to politicians and is often overly critical of female Parliamentarians in particular. It was agreed that there is a need to sensitize the media to the fact that the content of their reports and their method of reporting may harm not only the person being reported on but also the institution of Parliament as a whole.

There was a suggestion that there may be avenues for women MPs and media personalities to network in larger parliaments on the basis of common interests and concerns. Indeed it was pointed out that female MPs in some parliaments have promoted the establishment of a Women's Press Group. There was also support for the recommendation that female MPs should arrange media training sessions to bridge the gap and gain insight into how the media operates, network with media personnel and identify those media personalities who are sympathetic to gender issues.

There was a view that new political entrants and particularly female recruits are often not associated with autocratic practices and politicking, but rather are seen as symbols of honesty and caring – the latter being a characteristic that the television medium is best able to project. In this regard it was recommended that women Parliamentarians should take full advantage of any opportunity to utilize this form of media. It was noted that in some countries community television is more readily available for use than the mainstream press.

Conclusion

The Study Group concluded by recognizing that, although there are exceptions, generally the sole voices speaking out for women's rights and concerns are women. Women's rights are human rights. Therefore, it held that the active participation of women in Parliament is the only way to ensure that equality for women everywhere is achieved. However, it was universally agreed that co-operation between women and men is essential in any attempt at gender-sensitizing parliaments and removing the barriers which inhibit fullest participation by women. Many participants acknowledged that support from influential men has proven to be useful in the political struggle that women face on a daily basis.

In order to increase the effectiveness of female Parliamentarians, it was suggested that:

- Political parties must be encouraged to nominate women for winnable seats in the legislature, to train and initiate them to the workings of the legislature and to appoint them to prominent legislative and governmental positions.
- Cultural barriers can only be removed through efforts geared towards gender-awareness and, wherever necessary, by positive action by way of legislation.
- Parliamentary institutions must sponsor regular training and orientation sessions for their Members, amend their standing orders so that male-oriented terms are replace by inclusive language, and make women-friendly changes to their seating and other physical arrangements.
- Female Parliamentarians should promote the appointment of women to key positions within the legislature and the government; work at cross-party levels for the benefit of women as well as the wider society, and provide guidance and support to newer entrants; and
- Good working relationships with the media should be fostered.

The Study Group recommended the following areas for priority action:

1. Commonwealth parliaments should be urged to commit to gender-based analyses of all parliamentary documents, including policy proposals, legislation and committee reports, in order to assess their impact on the lives of women and men and to ensure that government policies, programmes and legislation are equitable for both women and men.
2. Commonwealth parliaments should be encouraged to consider introducing maternity and paternity benefits for Parliamentarians.
3. Proper facilities for the care of infants and young children should be established in Parliament buildings.
4. In those countries where, because of size and distance, it is necessary for MPs to utilize temporary accommodation nearer to Parlia-

ment, the parliamentary week should be narrowed with Parliament, if needed, sitting longer hours.

5. Where applicable, Constituency Weeks should be free of committee work, removing the requirement for MPs to travel away from their home territories and constituencies during such weeks. Where possible they should coincide with school holidays.
6. Commonwealth parliaments should be urged to be more flexible in the amount of time off allowed for family purposes and where possible, the good convention of pairing should be introduced for dealing with necessary absences by MPs.
7. Training and orientation programmes, sponsored by parliaments and involving both men and women, should be held on a regular basis throughout each parliamentary session, to assist MPs in a wide range of areas related to their functioning as Members of Parliament.
8. Concerted efforts must be made to ensure that women are appointed to prominent government offices and to serve on, as well as chair, important committees.
9. The standing orders should be regularly reviewed and, whenever necessary, amended, to ensure that the presence of women and issues pertaining to women are taken into account by parliaments, in order to encourage greater participation by women in the parliamentary process.
10. Female Parliamentarians should get together to discuss issues common to women. Toward this end, formal and informal women's networks should be set up within parliaments and women should identify policy issues where cross-party co-operation can exist.
11. As an inter-party grouping, female Parliamentarians should work with the various groups in society, for example non-governmental women's organizations and (community) radio and television, to promote awareness by the population of gender-sensitizing issues and create the environment for wider public support.
12. The CPA should encourage all Branches to be mindful of the fact that women should represent at least 30 per cent of its Executive Committee.
13. The CPA should reintroduce funding for meetings of the CWP Steering Committee.
14. The CPA should monitor the extent to which member branches fulfil their international obligations pertaining to the rights of women.

Notes

1 Reeta Chakrabarti, *Independent*, 25 January 2000.
2 As at March 2001. Source www.cpa.org.
3 *Gender-Based Analysis: A Quick Guide to Policy-Makers, Status of Women, Canada* (www.swc-cfc.gc.ca/publish/gbabro-e.html).

MEMBERS OF THE STUDY GROUP

	Region
Hon. Margaret Alva, MP (India)	Asia
Mrs Susan Barnes, MP (Canada)	Canada
Hon. Irene Chisala, MP (Zambia)	Africa
Miss Jennifer Edwards, MP (Jamaica)	Caribbean, Americas and the Atlantic
Hon. Hazel Hannan, MHK (Isle of Man)	British Isles and the Mediterranean
Datuk Napsiah Binti Omar, MP (Malaysia)	South-East Asia
Hon. Caroline Schaefer, MLC (South Australia)	Australia
Mrs Dianne Yates, MP (New Zealand)	The Pacific

Advisers

Sen. Dato' Ghazi H. Ramli (Malaysia)
Mrs Paula Kokkonen, MP (Finland)

In attendance

Ms Tuula Sivonen, Senior Clerk of Parliament (Finland)

Rapporteur

Mrs Jacqui Sampson-Jacent, Clerk of the House of Representatives (Trinidad and Tobago)

CPA Secretariat

Mr Raja Gomez (Director of Development and Planning)
Mr Anthony Staddon (Assistant Director of Development and Planning)

23 Gender-sensitizing Commonwealth parliaments: Commonwealth Parliamentary Conference Plenary Report, September 2001[1]

Commonwealth parliaments must bring in more women Members and make their proceedings more family-friendly because their societies need to mobilize all the strengths and skills of their communities to face contemporary challenges, said Dr Lesley Clark, MLA of the Australian state of Queensland.

In opening the third segment of the first plenary session of the Commonwealth Parliamentary Conference meeting in the Parliament of Australia in Canberra, Dr Clark said that a transformation of Parliament was necessary for the institution to regain the public confidence it had lost throughout the Commonwealth. Parliamentarians had to move beyond petty point-scoring to reassess their own roles as part of a reversal of the decline in public trust seen in Australia and elsewhere. A quarter of a century ago, opinion polling in Australia indicated 90 per cent of respondents trusted their Commonwealth MPs; today, that figure had plummeted to 10 per cent, she said.

Representation By Women

Dr Clark noted that the Commonwealth target of having 30 per cent of parliamentary seats held by women by 2005 could now only be achieved through affirmative action programmes. The Commonwealth total was now 14 per cent. On a regional basis, Africa stood at 15.5 per cent, Asia at 5.8 per cent, the British Isles and Mediterranean parliaments and legislatures at 18.6 per cent, Canadian Houses at 22 per cent, Caribbean assemblies at 17.5 per cent, Pacific parliaments at 8.7 per cent and assemblies in South-East Asia at 8.5 per cent.

The Queenslander said research showed that bringing more women into Parliament would improve governance as women were more honest, more co-operative, more aware of social problems, less likely to be self-serving and more able to deal with issues directly affecting women. However, she stressed that women were not saints, and setting such high expectations for them was only setting them up to fail.

However, she said the task of reforming and strengthening democratic institutions required good men and women to work together. In Australia, a Women's Charter for Political Reform had been drafted to help in the campaign to increase the numbers of women in the country's national, state and territorial houses and to reform the parliamentary system so it was no longer a male-oriented institution created by and for men, she said.

The goal was equality of representation between men and women both in parliaments and in governments. The presence of more women would reduce the levels of personal abuse now found in Australian houses, she said. She looked forward to the day when family facilities would be routinely available to all in all parliaments, women would be fully represented and gender inequality would no longer be an issue.

Dr Clark applauded the recommendations of a CPA Study Group on Gender-Sensitizing Commonwealth Parliaments that had reported earlier in the year. Family-friendly sitting hours and facilities, regular gender impact assessments on all policies, no gender discrimination in standing orders and more women MPs working together were suggested.

Dr Clark concluded that if men accepted the idea of more women in Parliament and if men and women were able to work together as equal partners in the political arena, the performance and reputation of parliamentary democracy would be greatly enhanced.

Opposing Views

Rt. Hon. Amaechi Rotimi, MLA, of Nigeria's Rivers State countered that the gender issue was being overdone. The real issue, he said, was unequal access to Parliament for all people, especially the poor.

He said that the prime focus of parliamentary reform programmes should be to remove the biases that meant that the men and women who did not have economic power could not have political power.

New Zealander Ms Georgina Beyer, JP, MP, noted that in her country women held all the top five public offices. She credited her country's mixed-member proportional representation system for increasing the opportunities for various groups, including women, to gain parliamentary seats. Political party candidate selection procedures were also key to the advancement of women, she said.

Acknowledging that party systems could easily increase the number of women elected, Mr Philip Braidwood, MHK, of the Isle of Man asked how this could be accomplished by non-party systems such as that of his jurisdiction, where it was up to women to stand and up to the voters to elect them.

He agreed that gender equity was desirable in Parliament, however, and suggested that education programmes, such as holding Youth Parliaments, could seek to prepare and encourage women to stand for office.

Affirmative action was also ruled out by Nigerian Parliamentarian Sen. Florence Ita-Giwa, who said force would not help to reverse the under-representation of women in African assemblies. She advocated that women enlist the support of men by convincing them that women were not their political enemies and that women could complement the contributions of men in the parliamentary arena.

Note

1 Gender-Sensitizing Parliaments in the Commonwealth, 47th Commonwealth Parliamentary Conference, First Plenary, Subject C – 10 September 2001.

24 Report of a Commonwealth Parliamentary Conference Workshop on Gender, September 2001[1]

The Chair, Dr Lesley Clark, MLA (Queensland) opened the workshop by commending the work of the Study Group set up in Kuala Lumpur in February and March 2001 to identify how barriers to the participation of women in public life could be overcome. The product of the working group, the report entitled *Gender-Sensitizing Commonwealth Parliaments*, was to be the focus of the workshop. Dr Clark particularly welcomed the large number of men in attendance, and encouraged all participants to actively contribute to the deliberations. The first paper was presented by Hon. Mario Galea, MP (Malta), who began by questioning whether the target set by the Commonwealth to have 30 per cent of women in decision-making positions by 2005 was achievable. He surmised that while some countries have already achieved this target, for others it would be extremely difficult if not impossible. Mr Galea saw great irony in the fact that in many parliaments the practices and procedures actively excluded women from the process, even in the name of democracy.

The inequality in areas of economics and education are most relevant, particularly as there are studies showing a direct correlation between higher levels of women representation and lower crime and corruption rates and less poverty. He raised the issue of an emerging form of illiteracy – computer illiteracy – and quoted

Canadian statistics that showed twice as many men used the Internet as did women. Mr Galea also presented some interesting statistics on the awarding of the Nobel prizes to demonstrate that while gender discrimination is recognized as unacceptable, sometimes it is unexpected. For instance, of the 400 awards for science and medicine, only eleven have gone to women, in the case of Madame Curie, twice, and on eight occasions it was shared. Statistics for the other categories are similar.

Mr Galea encouraged participants to widen their considerations: to look at how to encourage women to participate in processes that have so long excluded them, and to consider whether gay MPs should be included in the gender-sensitizing issue and future CPA deliberations. He ended by suggesting people give consideration to broader options such as establishment of a second chamber in which representation is based not on locality or constituency, but on terms of social function. The result could be a chamber that is more gender balanced and achieved without recourse to the more controversial option of affirmative action.

The second speaker, Hon. Zippora J. Kittony, MP (Kenya), outlined the situation in Kenya and proposed several strategies to move ahead. She noted that the Commonwealth Women Parliamentarian sessions held earlier in the day had shown that there was still much to be done, despite the good work of the Study Group and the enthusiasm of current delegates.

She sees the major goals, particularly in parts of Africa, as being the need to sensitize the whole electorate and to set realistic gender-sensitive goals for girls and boys, women and men. Explaining that Kenyan politics was more ethnic-based than issue-oriented, she outlined practices whereby women were manipulated by men with false promises of a gender-sensitive agenda, which were promptly abandoned once the men were elected by the voting power of these women. In Ms Kittoney's view it will take all sectors of the community working together to gender sensitize such an electorate and it has to include men as well as women. She cautioned that care must be taken to ensure that the people being supported for election are gender-sensitive and willing to work to further the agenda. While acknowledging that the situation in the Kenyan Parliament is unsatisfactory, she was heartened to note that the situation in the broader public and private sectors is more encouraging.

The third facilitator was Mrs Sue Barnes, MP (Canada), a member of the Study Group. Mrs Barnes posed some challenging questions on the actual performance of governments against treaties on inclusiveness and representation, signed by all but eight Commonwealth countries. She noted that the 2 per cent increase in women representation in twenty-five years hardly represented good progress, and saw the challenge as being the need to bring objectives to reality. She cautioned delegates that equality and equity is not the same thing and that often equity means applying resources to get equality.

Mrs Barnes pointed out that women were not clones of each other and that they will not automatically agree on every point. There is a need to acknowledge the individual starting points and progress from there. The strategies have been laid out and what is needed now is political will. She went on to outline the deliberations of the Study Group, which had agreed that women do make a difference to the ambience and procedures and do affect the type of legislation enacted. However, she agreed with Ms Kittoney that it was not just about getting women elected, but also about the outcomes arising from women being elected. She advised that the Study Group had concluded that there was a leadership role for the CPA to take and they have been encouraged by the support received from the Executive Committee and Secretariat. In this regard, all delegates were encouraged to use and promote the report in the way best suited to their jurisdictions to achieve the common goal of attracting and retaining more women Parliamentarians.

The workshop continued with contributions from a further twenty-five delegates who acknowledged the contributions of the facilitators and expressed their strong support for the report. While there were a range of views expressed based on the individual's situation and experiences, there were several common themes running through the presentations.

Some delegates saw a need to look deeper than gender equality strategies. The Hon. Mahayana Malose Anna Nyama, MPL (Northern Province) considered that the education and training of presiding officers was important to ensure that they understood the expectations of the different sexes and were equipped to promote gender-sensitive practices in their chambers. The Hon. Dato' Shahrizat Abdul Jalil, MP (Malaysia) also saw a need to reform institutions and address deficiencies in parliamentary processes and forums. She considered Malaysia to be a good example of what can be done and hoped it would encourage reform in other jurisdictions.

Ms N. Khumalo (Zimbabwe) considered that the impact of numbers depended on the type of assembly in place and suggested it would be better to look beyond numbers and consider how women can be more effective. Some delegates, including Ms Aneesa Ahmed (Maldives) quoted constitution and distance as barriers to the imposition of quota systems and preferred to adopt gender-sensitization strategies and encourage other women to enter politics through the provision of role models. Distance was an issue raised by Therese McCarthy Fagagamanualii (Samoa), who also encountered cultural barriers.

However other delegates supported quotas, and Ms Annette Ellis, MP (Australia) outlined how this had been implemented in her party with positive and improving results. The Hon. Hope Ruhindi Mwesigye, MP (Uganda) considered quotas should be extended to assist representation for all minority groups.

The need for women to encourage and support other women was a common issue raised by the delegates including the Hon. Vaaiga Paotama Tukuitonga (Niue). Ms Georgina Beyer, MP, JP (New Zealand) suggested that the rights of gay Parliamentarians also needed to be included in CWP and CPA deliberations The need to introduce more family-friendly strategies was echoed by many delegates. The Hon. Ponhele Ya France, MP (Namibia) outlined how the timing of proceedings, lack of transport and childcare facilities and concerns about safety can restrict women's participation.

The Hon. Mapheello Ts'uluba, MP (Lesotho) suggested that a start needed to be made within political parties, a sentiment supported by several delegates including Sen. Joan Yuille-Williams (Trinidad and Tobago), who saw a need to involve men in all forums discussing women and gender issues. In concert with other delegates, she also saw education as very important and strongly advocated better disaggregation and analysis of statistical information. Sen. Dato' Ghazi Ramli, (Malaysia) encouraged delegates to concentrate on making recommendations on how to take the report forward.

Picking up on issues raised by the facilitators, the Hon. Irene Chisala, MP (Zambia) questioned the progress by African nations to ensure treaty commitments were honoured. In Zambia, political parties were making executive positions available but gender seminars were poorly attended.

Sen. Ann Bailhache (Jersey) advised that Jersey had the largest number of working women in Europe and nineteen parliamentary representatives. There was a programme in place to help women contest elections but more work was needed in the civil service and private sector. Similar concerns were raised by Eleanor Burnham, AM (Wales).

Some delegates considered that there had been progress in support for women's representation through administrative and legislative reforms. Shri Suresh Chandal, MP (India) advised that India was committed to gender equality and that there were laws, development plans and programmes in place aimed at women's advancement. In addition the states were empowered to adopt measures of positive discrimination. The initiatives have been successful in encouraging participation in rural and urban areas, and steps are being taken aimed at increasing representation in the Lok Sabha from the current 5.3 per cent.

A similar picture was given by the Hon. Michael Rabereng Tshipinare, MP (Botswana), who advised that women had equal pay and paid maternity leave and many occupied high office. However parliamentary representation was only 18 per cent and other avenues needed to be pursued. The Hon. Terry E Lister, JP, MP (Bermuda) advised that while women had better education opportunities and were always the preferred target of opinion surveys, the barrier was the poor pay levels of Parliamentarians generally. This deterred young women already drawing higher salaries, and steps needed to be taken to make them willing to contribute.

The Hon. Lindiwe Maseko, MPL (Gauteng) outlined the positive initiatives taken to encourage women's participation including childcare, positive discrimination in party positions and legislative changes. She saw value in encouraging CHOGM to impose penalties where the 50 per cent representation target was not met. The value of sanctions was questioned by Robert P. Braidwood, MHK (Isle of Man) and by Mrs Sun Paranjothy (Observer, IPPF-ESEAOR), who preferred to address why the target had not been met.

The involvement of CHOGM in the implementation of the report was suggested by the Hon. Mahlubandile Dickson Qwase (Eastern Cape), who also supported the call for improved monitoring. The need to take stronger action to ensure promotion of the report and implementation of the finding was also raised by Thembmkosi Willies McHunu (Kwazulu-Natal), who saw this as the most pressing issue.

Smt. Margaret Alva (India) was the final speaker, and reiterated many of the concerns raised ahead of her including the continued lack of representation despite the apparent rate of progress; the allocation by men of a narrow range of jobs perceived to be relevant to women; the need for affirmative action and resources; the need to recast power structures, and the need to move ahead in partnership with men.

Dr Clark thanked all participants for the valuable contributions and supported the call for increased efforts to promote and implement the report, particularly the welcome recommendation for the future involvement of the CPA and Commonwealth Heads of Government.

Note

1 Gender-Sensitizing Parliaments in the Commonwealth, 47th Commonwealth Parliamentary Conference, Workshop C – 11 September 2001.
Chair: Dr Lesley Clark, MLA. Queensland
Panel: Hon. Mario Galea, MP, Malta
Hon. Zippora J. Kittony, MP, Kenya
Mrs Susan Barnes, MP, Canada

25 Strategic partnerships for politics in the twenty-first century: report of a Commonwealth Women Parliamentarians Meeting, September 2001[1]

The 13th meeting of Commonwealth Women Parliamentarians took place at Parliament House, Canberra, on 11 September 2001. The CWP Steering Committee Chairperson, Dr Lesley Clark, MLA (Queensland), chaired the breakfast meeting, which was attended by five members of the Steering Committee: CPA Secretary-General Mr Arthur Donahoe, CPA President Sen. the Hon. Margaret Reid of Australia, CPA Executive Committee Chairman Hon. Pius Msekwa, MP, of Tanzania, and CPA Vice-Chairman Hon. O'Love Jacobsen of Niue.

After a brief welcome by Dr Clark, the Hon. Caroline Schaefer, MLC (South Australia) presented a report back from the CPA Study Group on Gender-Sensitizing Commonwealth parliaments, which met in Kuala Lumpur, Malaysia, in February 2000. She began her report by acknowledging the difficulties in achieving recommendations that recognized the cultural diversity of the Commonwealth countries. Nevertheless, a number of recommendations had been made, and she encouraged male and female delegates to read the report and ensure that it was widely distributed across the CPA.

The next item on the agenda concerned funding of the Steering Committee for 2002. Dr Clark announced that the Executive

Committee had resolved to again make funding available so that the senior members of the Steering Committee could have a meeting at the time of the annual conference. It was considered preferable, however, for the Branch to nominate the senior Steering Committee member as a formal delegate with voting rights, rather than attending as an observer.

The CWP Meeting noted that there were two gender projects planned for 2002 – a workshop in West Africa on Gender, Politics and Conflict and a revised CWP leaflet which would publicize the work of the women's caucus.

CWP representation on the Executive Committee

The main focus of the business meeting concerned the motions put forward by Wales Branch to the CPA General Assembly which were aimed at achieving 30 per cent female membership of the CPA Executive Committee. Dr Clark expressed her hope that consensus could be achieved on this issue which would enable her to inform the General Assembly of the view of the CWP. She applauded the Executive Committee for its commitment to monitor actively and report on the progress of branches with respect to their support for women as conference delegates and members of the CPA Executive Committee.

The Secretary-General informed delegates that the Executive Committee's response to the two motions went a long way in his view towards achieving the aims that were implicit in what the Wales Branch, and many other Members of the CWP, had put forward. The CWP had to operate within the confines of the current constitution of the CPA, which did not allow for a reserved place on the Executive Committee for the CWP. If there were a desire on the part of the CWP to amend the constitution, it would have to be done through a mechanism of having a branch propose an amendment to the constitution. This was not on the agenda of this year's general assembly; the current issue was whether the CWP considered that the responses from the Executive Committee were reasonable, appropriate and met the objectives of the motions put forward by Wales Branch.

He ended his remarks by saying that it had been a great pleasure for him to work with so many dedicated members of the

CWP during his nine years as Secretary-General. He hoped that the CWP would strengthen and become an even more active participant in the affairs of the CPA in the future.

CWP members then discussed a draft response to the Wales motion. The Hon. Naledi Pandor, MP (South Africa) explained that the process of amending the CPA constitution would come through the appropriate channels as provided in the current constitution. What was necessary, she argued, was for the CWP to formulate proposed amendments to the constitution and for the Steering Committee to work out rules of procedure for itself.

Mrs Margaret Alva, MP (India) and Ms Georgina Beyer, MP (New Zealand) referred to the differences in the status of women within the regions of the CPA. In their view, an automatic place on the Executive Committee was required, no matter how many women were elected from the CPA regions. They were supported by Sen. Joan Yuille-Williams (Trinidad and Tobago) and Smt. Ambika Soni, MP (India), who both suggested putting forward a motion for constitutional change to ensure that the CWP chairperson was a Member of the Executive Committee.

Smt. Soni argued that the CWP needed to be radical to show that it was determined to achieve change, while Ms Beyer said that women had a valuable contribution to make to the CPA. However, the assertiveness of women was unfortunately sometimes mistaken for some form of aggression. Smt. Renuka Chowdhury, MP (India) agreed that the mindset of men had to be changed.

A delegate from Jersey, Senator Ann Bailhache, expressed concern that a reserved place on the Executive Committee for the CWP Chair would result in branches nominating fewer women to the Executive Committee. Ms Kate Kainja, MP (Malawi) thought there were two issues arising from the two motions: first, how women can increase their representation in parliaments, and second, how to increase the representation of women on the Executive Committee. In her view, the first issue was more important.

Mrs Sue Barnes, MP (Canada) agreed that it was important for the CWP to be constructive and inclusive, and suggested that the priority should be for the CWP to enter the structures of the CPA in a more formalized way. After lengthy discussion on the terms of the CWP response to the Wales Branch motions and Executive Committee report, the following response was agreed:

1. The CWP commended the Wales Branch for its motions that aim to achieve 30 per cent of women on the CPA Executive Committee and ensure that the perspective of women Parliamentarians is fully considered by the CPA.
2. The CWP thanked the CPA Executive Committee for their comprehensive and considered response to the Wales Branch motions. The Six Point Plan adopted by the Executive Committee brings forward proposals to work towards the goal of 30 per cent women on the Executive Committee one year earlier than requested by Wales Branch motion 1.
3. The CWP also recognized that the Six Point Plan accommodates recommendations (l) and (m) of the report of the CPA Study Group on Gender-Sensitizing Commonwealth Parliaments, namely (l) The CPA should encourage all branches to be mindful of the fact that women should represent at least 30 per cent of its Executive Committee, and (m) The CPA should reintroduce funding for meetings of the CWP Steering Committee.
4. The CWP also welcomed the proposal of the Executive Committee to actively monitor and report on the progress of branches with respect to their support for women as conference delegates and members of the CPA Executive Committee.
5. Members of the CWP reserved their right to bring forward new motions to the general assembly proposing changes in the constitution of the CPA to enable the CWP Chairperson to become a member of the Executive Committee.
6. The CWP commended the CPA for its decision to update the CWP leaflet but requested that the CPA increase its efforts to raise the profile of the CWP and the work of its Members through regular inserts into its journal, *The Parliamentarian*, and an interactive section of the CPA Website.

CWP Plenary Meeting

Dr Lesley Clark welcomed delegates to the plenary meeting and especially the men who had joined the group, given that the theme for the session was partnerships. She expressed pleasure at the particularly good attendance at the previous business session and the progress that had been made in considering the draft response to the Executive Committee on the Wales motion. Dr Clark introduced Senator the Hon. Amanda Vanstone (Australia), Minister for Family and Community Services and Minister advising the Prime Minister for the Status of Women.

Senator Vanstone expressed the view that an effective democracy meant that all voices are heard. Although New Zealand had been the first country to give women the vote, Australia was the first to let women vote and stand for Parliament; however it took twenty years for the first woman to be elected. Since that time the situation had improved, and representation across Australian Legislatures ranged from 37.1 per cent in Queensland to eleven Legislatures in the Australian Capital Territory. Senator Vanstone cautioned against using statistics, explaining that these often showed details about women of status not about the status of women.

During her address, she remarked that the democratic process was enhanced by the participation of women. However, experience showed that it took a long time to effect changes for women in the home and positive assistance, such as improved access to childcare facilities, education and financial support, was necessary. In conclusion, the Senator praised the efforts of women who had gone before, particularly grandmothers who were now being asked to take on another job, minding the children of the next generation of women in decision-making roles.

The meeting then split into regional workshops to address a small number of issues that would lead to enhanced democracy or improvement in parliamentary practices that benefit both men and women.

Asia and South-East Asia Regions

Convenor: Mrs Margaret Alva, MP (India)
Reporter: Hon. Dato' Shahrizat Abdul Jalil, MP (Malaysia)

Following some fruitful discussion on the situation in the regions, the group came to the following conclusions:

- While affirmative action had been taken, there were social, cultural and religious barriers and economic disparities that required additional empowerment processes to enable participation in actual decision-making.

- There was a need to ensure legislation is more equitable and just towards women.
- Roles of men and women in the home, in society and in the work-place need to be redefined.
- The workplace environment should be sensitized to ensure women's participation as equal partners.
- Affirmative action was required to ensure women's access to justice and the elimination of economic exploitation and social oppression.

Africa Region

Convenor: Hon. Irene Chisala, MP (Zambia)
Reporter: Senator Florence Ita-Giwa (Nigeria)

Senator Ita-Giwa reflected that participants in the Africa regional workshop all brought diverse experiences due to cultural and religious differences. However, agreement was reached on certain points:

- Women were happy to work in partnership with men to achieve 30 per cent representation.
- There was a need for women in leadership positions to encourage and convince the women of the next generation that the days when women needed to fight the men to achieve success were gone.
- Women should make use of NGOs and form bodies in which they were able to encourage more women to participate.
- Affirmative action would help more women into Parliament and into positions of power.

CWP Members reported that they were very keen on working on these ideas further in future CPA events in the Africa region.

Canada and British Islands and Mediterranean Regions

Convenor: Mrs Cheryl Gillan, MP (UK)
Reporter: Mrs Sarmite Bulte, MP (Canada)

Several key conclusions emerged from the discussions:

- Political will at the party level was key, as was starting at the grass roots: it was easier to start from scratch, as illustrated by the Scottish and Welsh Assemblies where the representation of women is extremely high.
- Legislation that allows parties to positively discriminate and to appoint women in certain constituencies was important.
- Gender analysis and mainstreaming was also very important: analysing legislation for its affect on men and women was crucial, but it was felt that this should be done at the draft stage.
- Mentoring assistance was felt to be very important, as was training for both male and female politicians.
- Financial assistance, such as found through Emily's List in the UK or the Judy LaMarsh Fund in Canada which gives each nominated woman $2,000, win or lose, was important.
- Under the leadership of Prime Minister Pierre Elliott Trudeau, Canada had introduced the Charter of Rights and Freedoms, which entrenched rights into the constitution and ensured that women were not discriminated against.
- It was agreed that women were consensus builders who tend to work harder and faster, enabling legislation to progress more quickly, and although all issues interest women, there were certain issues that women can better bring forward.
- An important change needed to improve democracy was parliamentary reform – increasing the role of the individual member and also increasing the effectiveness of the opposition.
- Partnerships with the media, and learning to work with the media.
- The gender digital divide was also addressed: in Canada only 25 per cent of women know how to use a computer, and though 58 per cent of women hold university degrees, only 10 to 15 per cent look for careers in science and technology and engineering.

The group made reference to a recent World Bank report called Engendering Development: Through Gender Equality in Rights, Resources and Voice, which found that greater participation of women in the political and economic structures of their economies was associated with more effective development, including lower levels of corruption and better governance.

Australia and Pacific Regions

Convenor and Reporter: Hon. Caroline Schaefer, MLC (South Australia)

The theme that emerged during this workshop was the need to have more women in Parliament. In Papua New Guinea only two Members out of 109 are women and consideration was being given to appointing more women, having women-only seats or moving to open competition. While not seen as having universal application, it was acknowledged that in some countries at least appointing women to Parliament had worked very well.

There were a number of areas raised that the group believed to have been helpful. The Australian Labor Party internal rule that by 2002 35 per cent of people pre-selected must be women was believed to have shifted some entrenched values. Again, Emily's List was raised as a success story, as well as the various other internal party political methods of raising money and mentoring females, using male and female colleagues.

In conclusion, the strong message was the need first of all to concentrate on getting women into Parliament and then making the cultural and structural changes. Some Members believed that women were not necessarily able to stand for Parliament until they were older and their families more established.

Caribbean, Americas and Atlantic region

Convenor and Reporter: Ms Patricia J. Gordon-Pamplin, JP, MP (Bermuda)

It was agreed that women needed to be assertive enough to grasp the political opportunities available to them. One delegate advised that there was difficulty with the mindset of men with respect to them accepting the value of women in politics. There was discussion on the issue that some appointments given to women were being made as a result of political expediency and not necessarily as a result of ability.

Another issue explored was that of proportional representation which was felt by some to enhance the balance that exists between women and men in the political arena. Economic empowerment of women in order to facilitate their entry into the political arena and mentoring female parliamentarians to ensure that new Members of Parliament have somebody to whom they can relate were also discussed. Under the theme 'justice and democracy', fairness in sentencing was addressed because domestic violence within the Caribbean area is a major problem.

The Chair, Dr Lesley Clark, MLA (Queensland) thanked the delegates and the reporters and commented that some common themes had emerged. She acknowledged the point that partnerships must begin in the home, and that those partnerships were perhaps the place to get the changes in attitude that are needed if women are to make successful partnerships in other institutions they are involved in, including the Parliament.

There was consensus in all groups that the case for equal partnerships can be best argued using the following themes:

- justice and democracy (women make up 50 per cent of the population)
- efficiency (the waste of huge resources of talent and creativity), and
- women contribute different skills and styles to enrich democratic politics.

In the spirit of partnership with men, Dr Clark invited male delegates to contribute their views. Mr Jackson Muvangila Makwetta, MP (Tanzania) congratulated the women for their diplomatic and carefully analysed approach to issues, and emphasized the need to work together. Mr Brian Donnelly, MP (New Zealand) advised that in New Zealand women were involved in politics because they had the qualities to do the job and were respected by men on that basis. The Hon. Michael Summers, MLC advised that the equality in his Falkland Islands has resulted in the possibility of 50 per cent representation in the next Parliament, but he cautioned against promoting the idea that women work harder or better than men. He suggested that it would be worth assessing whether there may be a relationship between high numbers of women police and lower rates of domestic violence. Similarly, Mr Peter Pike, MP (United Kingdom) cautioned against saying men's issues were for men to discuss and vice versa. He supported increasing the number of women in Parliament, but raised the issue of ensuring all other sectors of the community were represented.

The meeting was then opened up to more general discussion and the Hon. Naledi Pandor, MP (South Africa) identified several areas she thought were worth pursuing, starting with the need for the role of elected representatives to go beyond ensuring the presence of women in Parliament and to look at all institutions in a society. Another issue was the importance of political parties and the role they play in determining the final participation of women in politics. The Hon. Lindiwe Maseko, MPL (Gauteng) raised the issue of the lack of childcare facilities at CPA conferences and sought to have this policy changed.

Sen. Gillian Lucky (Trinidad and Tobago) agreed with the men who had raised concerns about separating the efforts of men and women, but pointed out that this often arose because women needed to work harder to achieve the same level of recognition. She also suggested that gender-sensitization began in the home and discussed the role of men in supporting women in their endeavours. Ms Lucky saw a need for successful women to help other women and to be more supportive. She was also concerned that affirmative action could result in an attitude that a woman had been given a job and not earned it.

Dr Lesley Clark ended the session by congratulating and thanking all those who had made this a successful session of CWP through their hard work and contributions. She reminded delegates that the test of the value of what had been done was taking the results and ideas back to the regions, to the parliaments and to the organizations that they are involved in and implementing them.

Note

1 47th Commonwealth Parliamentary Conference, Canberra, Australia, 11 September 2001.

26 Representation of Women in Commonwealth parliaments and legislatures

The following tables contain figures from a wide selection of Commonwealth parliaments and legislatures, by geographical regions, which show the number of seats in various houses and the number of women who occupy some of those seats. The lists of houses, as provided by the Commonwealth Parliamentary Association, are not exhaustive, and no such list can ever be completely up to date, given the frequency of elections and by-elections. But the data does provide a snapshot of the extent to which women occupy Commonwealth parliamentary and legislative seats at the beginning of the twenty-first century.

Table 26.1 Female representation in various houses: Africa

Branch	*Chamber*	*Seats*	*Women*	*%*
Cameroon	National Assembly	180	9	5
Gambia	House Of Reps	49	1	2.0
Ghana	Parliament	200	19	9.5
Kenya	National Assembly	224	9	4.0
Lesotho	National Assembly	80	2	2.5
Lesotho	Senate	33	10	30.3
Malawi	National Assembly	193	18	9.3
Mauritius	National Assembly	70	4	5.7
Mozambique	Assembly Of The Republic	250	75	30
Namibia	National Assembly	78	18	23.1

Table 26.1 Female representation in various houses: Africa – *continued*

Branch	*Chamber*	*Seats*	*Women*	*%*
Namibia	National Council	26	2	7.7
Nigeria	House Of Representatives	360	14	3.9
Nigeria	Senate	108	4	3.7
Nigeria – Anambra	House Of Assembly	30	1	3.3
Nigeria – Benue	House Of Assembly	29	1	3.4
Nigeria – Borno	House Of Assembly	28	0	0
Nigeria – Edo	House Of Assembly	24	2	8.3
Nigeria – Enugu	House Of Assembly	24	0	0
Nigeria – Gombe	House Of Assembly	24	1	4.2
Nigeria – Niger	House Of Assembly	27	2	7.4
Seychelles	National Assembly	34	9	26.5
Sierra Leone	Parliament	80	8	10
South Africa	National Assembly	400	123	30.8
South Africa	National Council Of Provinces	90	18	20
South Africa – Eastern Cape	Provincial Legislature	63	15	23.8
South Africa – Free State	Provincial Legislature	30	7	23.3
South Africa – Gauteng	Provincial Legislature	76	25	32.9
South Africa – Kwazulu-Natal	Provincial Legislature	80	21	26.3
South Africa – Mpumalanga	Provincial Legislature	30	9	30
South Africa – Northern Cape	Provincial Legislature	30	9	30
South Africa – Northern Province	Provincial Legislature	49	15	30.6
South Africa – North-West	Provincial Legislature	33	10	30.3
South Africa – Western Cape	Provincial Legislature	42	9	21.4
Swaziland	House Of Assembly	65	4	6.2
Swaziland	Senate	30	5	16.7
Tanzania	National Assembly	295	63	21.4
Tanzania – Zanzibar	Legislative Assembly	76	13	17.1
Uganda	National Assembly	281	54	19.2
Zambia	National Assembly	158	15	9.5
Zimbabwe	Parliament	150	22	14.7

Table 26.2 Female representation in various houses: Asia

Branch	*Chamber*	*Seats*	*Women*	*%*
Bangladesh	Jatio Sangsad	300	6	2
India	Lok Sabha	550	49	8.9
India	Rajya Sabha	250	22	8.8
India – Andhra Pradesh	Legislative Assembly	295	34	11.5
India – Arunachal Pradesh	Legislative Assembly	60	1	1.7
India – Assam	Legislative Assembly	126	1	0.8
India – Bihar	Legislative Assembly	243	15	6.2
India – Bihar	Legislative Council	96	1	1.0
India – Delhi	Legislative Assembly	70	9	12.9
India – Goa	Legislative Assembly	40	1	2.5
India – Gujarat	Legislative Assembly	182	5	2.7
India – Haryana	Legislative Assembly	90	4	4.4
India – Himachal Pradesh	Legislative Assembly	68	6	8.8
India – Jammu And Kashmir	Legislative Assembly	87	2	2.3
India – Karnataka	Legislative Assembly	225	6	2.7
India – Karnataka	Legislative Council	75	7	9.3
India – Kerala	Legislative Assembly	141	13	9.2
India – Madhya Pradesh	Legislative Assembly	321	23	7.2
India – Maharashtra	Legislative Assembly	289	13	4.5
India – Maharashtra	Legislative Council	78	8	10.3
India – Manipur	Legislative Assembly	60	0	0
India – Meghalaya	Legislative Assembly	60	3	5
India – Mizoram	Legislative Assembly	40	0	0
India – Nagaland	Legislative Assembly	60	0	0
India – Punjab	Legislative Assembly	117	8	6.8
India – Rajasthan	Legislative Assembly	200	14	7
India – Sikkim	Legislative Assembly	32	1	3.1
India – Tamil Nadu	Legislative Assembly	235	31	13.2
India – Tripura	Legislative Assembly	60	3	5
India – Uttar Pradesh	Legislative Assembly	404	15	3.7
India – Uttar Pradesh	Legislative Council	108	3	2.8
India – West Bengal	Legislative Assembly	295	23	7.8
Maldives	Citizen's Majlis	48	5	10.4
Sri Lanka	Parliament	225	9	4

Table 26.3 Female representation in various houses: Australia

Branch	*Chamber*	*Seats*	*Women*	*%*
Australia	House of Reps	150	38	25.3
Australia	Senate	76	22	28.9
Australian Capital Territory	Legislative Assembly	17	6	35.3
New South Wales	Legislative Assembly	93	18	19.4
New South Wales	Legislative Council	42	10	23.8
Norfolk Island	Legislative Assembly	9	2	22.2
Northern Territory	Legislative Assembly	25	7	28
Queensland	Legislative Assembly	89	33	37.1
South Australia	House of Assembly	47	14	29.8
South Australia	Legislative Council	22	5	22.7
Tasmania	House of Assembly	25	7	28
Tasmania	Legislative Council	15	4	26.7
Victoria	Legislative Assembly	88	22	25
Victoria	Legislative Council	44	12	27.3
Western Australia	Legislative Assembly	57	13	22.8
Western Australia	Legislative Council	34	10	29.4

Table 26.4 Female representation in various houses: British Islands and Mediterranean

Branch	*Chamber*	*Seats*	*Women*	*%*
Alderney	States of Alderney	10	1	10
Cyprus	House of Reps	56	6	10.7
Falkland Islands	Legislative Council	8	3	37.5
Gibraltar	House of Assembly	18	2	11.1
Guernsey	States of Deliberation	57	9	15.8
Isle Of Man	House of Keys	24	3	12.5
Isle Of Man	Legislative Council	11	1	9.1
Jersey	States of Jersey	53	9	17.0
Malta	House of Reps	65	6	9.2
St Helena	Legislative Council	16	2	12.5
UK	House of Commons	659	118	17.9
UK	House of Lords	696	114	16.4
UK – Northern Ireland	Assembly	108	15	13.9
UK – Scotland	Scottish Parliament	129	48	37.2
UK – Wales	Welsh Assembly	60	26	43.3

Table 26.5 Female representation in various houses: Canada

Branch	*Chamber*	*Seats*	*Women*	*%*
Canada	House of Commons	301	62	20.6
Canada	Senate	105	33	31.5
Alberta	Legislative Assembly	83	16	19.3
British Columbia	Legislative Assembly	79	19	24.1
Manitoba	Legislative Assembly	57	14	24.6
New Brunswick	Legislative Assembly	55	10	18.2
Newfoundland	House of Assembly	48	8	16.7
Northwest Territories	Legislative Assembly	19	2	10.5
Nova Scotia	House of Assembly	52	4	7.7
Nunavut	Legislative Assembly	19	2	10.5
Ontario	Legislative Assembly	103	18	17.5
Prince Edward Island	Legislative Assembly	27	6	22.2
Quebec	National Assembly	125	31	24.8
Saskatchewan	Legislative Assembly	58	12	20.7
Yukon	Legislative Assembly	17	5	29.4

Table 26.6 Female representation in various houses: Caribbean, Atlantic and Americas

Branch	*Chamber*	*Seats*	*Women*	*%*
Anguilla	House Of Assembly	12	0	0
Antigua and Barbuda	House of Reps	17	1	5.9
Antigua and Barbuda	Senate	17	2	11.8
Bahamas	House of Assembly	40	6	15
Bahamas	Senate	16	6	37.5
Barbados	House of Assembly	28	3	10.7
Barbados	Senate	21	7	33.3
Belize	House of Reps	29	3	10.3
Belize	Senate	9	5	55.6
Bermuda	House of Assembly	40	8	20
Bermuda	Senate	11	2	18.2
British Virgin Islands	Legislative Council	15	2	13.3
Cayman Islands	Legislative Assembly	18	2	11.1
Dominica	House of Assembly	31	6	19.4
Grenada	House of Reps	15	4	26.7
Grenada	Senate	13	1	7.7
Guyana	National Assembly	65	12	18.5
Jamaica	House of Representatives	60	9	15
Jamaica	Senate	21	5	23.8
Montserrat	Legislative Council	12	3	25
St Kitts and Nevis	National Assembly	15	2	13.3
Nevis Island	Nevis Island Assembly	8	2	25
St Lucia	House of Assembly	18	2	11.1
St Lucia	Senate	11	3	27.3
St Vincent and the Grenadines	Legislative Assembly	15	5	33.3
Trinidad and Tobago	House of Reps	37	4	10.8
Trinidad and Tobago	Senate	31	10	32.6
Turks and Caicos Islands	Legislative Council	18	4	22.2

Table 26.7 Female representation in various houses: Pacific

Branch	*Chamber*	*Seats*	*Women*	*%*
Cook Islands	Parliament	25	1	4
Kiribati	Legislative Assembly	42	2	4.8
Nauru	Parliament	18	0	0
New Zealand	House of Reps	120	34	28.3
Niue	Legislative Assembly	20	37	10
Papua New Guinea	National Parliament	109	2	0.9
Samoa	Legislative Assembly	49	1	6.1
Solomon Islands	National Parliament	50	0	0
Tonga	Parliament	30	3	0
Tuvalu	Parliament	15	0	0
Vanuatu	Parliament	52	0	0

Table 26.8 Female representation in various houses: South-East Asia

Branch	*Chamber*	*Seats*	*Women*	*%*
Malaysia	Dewan Negara	69	21	30.4
Malaysia	Dewan Rakyat	193	20	10.4
Malaysia – Johore	Legislative Assembly	40	4	10
Malaysia – Kedah Darulaman	Legislative Assembly	36	3	8.3
Malaysia – Kelantan	Legislative Assembly	43	0	0
Malaysia – Malacca	Legislative Assembly	25	2	8
Malaysia – Negeri Sembilan	Legislative Assembly	32	2	6.3
Malaysia – Pahang	Legislative Assembly	38	2	5.3
Malaysia – Penang	Legislative Assembly	33	4	12.1
Malaysia – Perak	Legislative Assembly	53	2	3.8
Malaysia – Perlis	Legislative Assembly	15	1	6.7
Malaysia – Sabah	Legislative Assembly	54	2	3.7
Malaysia – Sarawak	Legislative Assembly	62	3	4.8
Malaysia – Selangor	Legislative Assembly	48	3	6.3
Malaysia – Terengganu	Legislative Assembly	32	0	0
Singapore	Parliament	85	10	11.8

Selected Bibliography and Useful Sources

Abrar, S. *et al.* (2000) 'Feminist ideas and domestic violence policy change', *Political Studies*, **48**.

Arouff-Parfait, Marie-Claude (1997) 'Gender equality: women's role in the modern political world', *The Parliamentarian*, **38**(3), pp. 26M–27M.

Bashevkin, Sylvia (1993) *Toeing the Lines: Women and Party Politics in English Canada,* 2nd edn, Oxford: Oxford University Press; ISBN 0195408500.

Bayes, Jane H. and Tohidi, Nayereh (eds) (2001) *Globalization, Gender, and Religion: The Politics of Women's Rights in Catholic and Muslim Contexts,* Basingstoke: Palgrave Macmillan.

Bergqvist, C. (1997) 'Sweden', in J. Lovenduski and S. Stephenson (eds), *State of the Art Study of Research on Women and Decision-Making in the EU,* Report to the European Commission.

Bergqvist, C. *et al.* (1999) *Equal Democracies? Gender and Politics in the Nordic Countries.*

Carby, H. (1982) 'White women listen! Black feminism and the boundaries of sisterhood', in CCCS (ed.), *The Empire Strikes Back: Race and Racism in 70s Britain*, London: Routledge.

Can-oil, S. J. and Zerilli, M. G. (1983) 'Feminist challenges to political science', in A. W. Finifter (ed.), *Political Science: The State of the Discipline,* Washington DC: American Political Science Association.

Carroll, S. J. (1985) *Women as Candidates in American Politics,* Bloomington, IN: Indiana University Press.

Clark, Dr Lesley (2001) 'Gender balance in parliament: which electoral system can best promote equitable representation by women?' *The Parliamentarian*, **82**(4), pp. 341–8.

Cockburn, C. (1991) *In the Way of Women: Men's Resistance to Sex Equality in Organisations*, Basingstoke: Macmillan.

Coleman, Stephen and Normann, Emilie (2000) *New Media and Social Inclusion*, London: Hansard Society.

Commonwealth Parliamentary Conference (2000) 'Addressing imbalances: Commonwealth women Parliamentarians and empowerment', *The Parliamentarian*, **81**(1), pp. 33–6.

Dahlerup, D. (1988) 'From a small to a large minority: women in Scandinavian politics', *Scandinavian Political Studies*, 11, pp. 275–98.

Dancz, Virginia H.(1987) *Women and Party Politics in Peninsular Malaysia*, Oxford: Oxford University Press; ISBN 0195826892.

Darcy, R., Welch, S. and Dark, J. (1987) *Women, Elections, and Representation*, New York: Longman.

Davis, Rebecca Howard (1997) *Women and Power in Parliamentary Democracies: Cabinet Appointments in Western Europe, 1968–1992*, Lincoln, NE: University of Nebraska Press; ISBN 0803217072.

Diamond, I. (1977) *Sex Roles in the State House*, New Haven, CT: Yale University Press.

Dodson, D. L. (1991) *Gender and Policymaking: Studies of Women in Office*, New Brunswick, NJ: Center for the American Woman and Politics.

Dodson, D. L. and Carroll, S. J. (1991) *Reshaping the Agenda: Women in State Legislatures,* New Brunswick NJ: Center for the American Woman and Politics.

Duerst-Lahti, G. and Kelly, R. M. (eds) (1995) *Gender Power, Leadership and Governance*, Ann Arbor, MI: University of Michigan Press.

Enloe, Cynthia (1993) *The Morning After*, Berkeley, CA: University of California Press.

Enloe, Cynthia (2001) *Bananas, Beaches and Bases*, 2nd edn, Berkeley, CA: University of California Press; ISBN 0520229126.

Evans, Richard J. (1979) *The Feminists*, London: Croom Helm.

Feminist Review (2002) Special issue on *Globalisation, Feminist Review,* **70**.

Flanz, Gisbert (1983) *Comparative Women's Rights and Political Participation in Europe*, Ardsley, NY: Transnational; ISBN 0941320022.

Freeman, J. (2000) *A Room at a Time: How Women Entered Party Politics*, Lanham, MD: Rowman and Littlefield.

Githens, M. (1983) 'The elusive paradigm gender, politics and political behavior: the state of the art', in A. W. Finifter (ed.), *Political Science: The State of the Discipline*, Washington DC: American Political Science Association.

Githens, M. and Prestage, J. L. (eds) (1977) *A Portrait of Marginality: The Political Behavior of the American Woman*, New York: McKay.

Haavio, Mannila *et al.* (1985) *Unfinished Democracy: Women in Nordic Politics*, Oxford: Pergamon.

Hearn, J. (1989) *The Sexuality of Organisation*, London: Sage.

Hoskyns, C.(1996) *Integrating Gender*, London: Verso.

Hunt, Victoria Carew (1998) *One Two One: Women in Parliament*, London: Politico.

Jennings, M. K. and Niemi, R. G. (1981) *Generations and Politics: A Panel Study of Young Adults and Their Parents*, Princeton, NJ: Princeton University Press.

Judge, D. (1999) *Representation: Theory and Practice in Britain*, London: Routledge.

Karvonnen, L. and Selle, P. (1995) *Women in Nordic Politics: Closing the Gap*, Aldershot: Dartmouth.

Kaplan, C., Alarcon, N. and Moallem, M. (1999) *Between Woman and Nation: Nationalisms, Transnational Feminisms, and the State*, Durham, NC: Duke University Press.

Karam, Azza et al. (1998) *Women in Parliament: Beyond Numbers*, Stockholm: International Idea; ISBN 9189098196 <http://www.idea.int/women/parl/toc.htm>.

Kelly, Rita Mae, Bayes, Jane, Hawkesworth, Mary and Young, Brigitte (eds) (2001) *Gender, Globalization, and Democratization*, Lanham, MD: Rowman and Littlefield; ISBN 0742509788.

Kenny, S. (1996) 'New research on gendered political institutions', *Political Research Quarterly*, **49**, pp. 445–63.

Kirkpatrick, J. J. (1974) *Political Woman*, New York: Basic Books.

Lewis, J. (1992) 'Gender and the development of welfare regimes', *Journal of European Social Policy*, **3**, pp. 159–73.

Lister, R. (1997) *Citizenship: Feminist Perspectives*, Basingstoke: Palgrave/Macmillan.

Lovecey, J. (2000) 'Des citoyennes à part entière': the parity reforms of 1999–2000 and the constitutionalisation of gendered citizenship in France', paper presented to the annual meeting of the Political Studies Association, London, April 2000.

Lovenduski, J. (1986) *Women and European Politics: Contemporary Feminism and Public Policy*, Brighton: Wheatsheaf.

Lovenduski, J. (1998) 'Gendering research in political science', *Annual Review of Political Science*, **1**, pp. 333–56.

Lovenduski, J. (1999) 'Sexing political behaviour in Britain', in S. Walby (ed.), *New Agendas for Women*, Basingstoke: Macmillan.

Lovenduski, Joni (2001) 'Women and politics: minority representation or critical mass?' *Parliamentary Affairs*, **54**(4), pp. 743–58.

Lovenduski, J. and Norris, P. (eds) (1993) *Gender and Party Politics*, London: Sage.

Lovenduski, Joni and Randall, Vicky (1993) *Contemporary Feminist Politics*, Oxford: Oxford University Press (especially Introduction and Conclusions).

Marchand, Marianne H. and Runyan, Anne Sisson (eds) (2000) *Gender and Global Restructuring*, London: Routledge.

McDougall, Linda (1998) *Westminster Women*, London: Vintage.

McGregor, Francis (2001) 'Women in politics: assuming a leadership role in Parliament and society', *The Parliamentarian*, **82**(3), pp. 265–7.

Medina, C. (1993) *Do International Human Rights Laws Protect Women?* London: Zed and North South Institute.

Midgley, Clare (1998) *Gender and Imperialism*, Manchester: Manchester University Press.

Nelson, Barbara and Chowdury, Najma (1994) (eds) *Women and Politics Worldwide*, New Haven, CT: Yale University Press.

Norris, P. and Lovenduski, J. (1995) *Political Recruitment: Gender, Race and Class in the British Parliament*, Cambridge: Cambridge University Press.

Orloff, A. (1996) 'Gender in the welfare state', *Annual Review of Sociology*, **22**, pp. 51–78.

Oyewumi, Oyeronke (ed.) (2002) *African Women and Feminism: Reflecting on the Politics of Sisterhood*, Lawrenceville, NJ: Africa World Press.

Patel, Pragna (1997) 'Third wave feminism and black women's activism', in Heidi Safia Mirza (ed.), *Black British Feminism: A Reader*, London: Routledge.

Pateman, C. (1988) *The Sexual Contract*, Cambridge: Polity.

Phillips, A. (1991) *Engendering Democracy*, Cambridge, UK: Polity.

Phillips, A. (1993) *Democracy and Difference,* Cambridge, UK: Polity.

Phillips, A. (1994) 'Democracy and representation, or why should it matter who our representatives are,' *Schweizerisches Jahrsbuchfür Politische Wissenschaft,* **3**, pp. 63–78.

Phillips, A. (1995) *The Politics of Presence,* Oxford: Oxford University Press.

Pitkin, H. (1967) *The Concept of Representation*, Berkeley: University of California Press.

Polidano, Charles and Manning, Nick (1996) 'Why civil service reforms fail', Public Policy Management Working Paper no. 16, University of Manchester Institute for Development Policy and Management.

Randall, V. (1987) *Women and Politics: An International Perspective,* 2nd edn, Basingstoke: Macmillan.

Sainsbury, D. (1996) *Gender Equality and Welfare States*, Cambridge: Cambridge University Press.

Sapiro, V. (1983) *The Political Integration of Women: Roles, Socialization, and Politics*, Urbana, IL: University of Illinois Press.

Sarker, Sonita and De, Esha Niyogi (eds) (2002) *Gender in the Globalization of South and Southeast Asia*, Durham, NC: Duke University Press.

Sawer, Marian (2000) 'Parliamentary representation of women: from discourses of justice to strategies of accountability', *International Political Science Review*, **21**(4), pp. 361–80.

Scott, J. (1997) '"La Querelle des Femmes" in the late twentieth century', *New Left Review*, **226**, pp. 3–20.

Sharoni, Simona (1994) *Gender and the Israeli-Palestinian Conflict: The Politics of Women's Resistance* (Syracuse Studies on Peace and Conflict Resolution), Syracuse, NY: Syracuse University Press.

Siaroff, Alan (2000) 'Women's representation in legislatures and cabinets in industrial democracies', *International Political Science Review*, **21**(2), pp. 197–215.

Sinha, Niraj (2000) *Women in Indian Politics: Empowerment of Women Through Political Participation*, New Delhi: Gyan; ISBN 8121206863.

Skjeie, H. (1991) 'The rhetoric of difference: on women's inclusion in political elites', *Politics and Society*, **2**.

Skjelsbaek, Inger and Smith, Dan (eds) (2001) *Gender, Peace and Conflict,* London: Sage.

Stetson, D. M. and Mazur, A. (1995) *Comparative State Feminism*, London: Sage.

Stivers, C. (1993) *Gender Images in Public Administration*, London: Sage.

Tibballs, Sue (2000) *The Sexual Renaissance*, Women's Communication Centre.

Tickner, J. Ann (1993) *Gender in International Relations*, New York: Columbia University Press.

Tickner, J. Ann (2001) *Gendering World Politics: Issues and Approaches in the Post-Cold War Era*, New York: Columbia University Press; ISBN 0231113676.

Tremblay, Manon (2000) 'Women, citizenship, and representation: an introduction', *International Political Science Review*, **21**(4), pp. 339–43.

Tremblay, Manon (2000) 'More feminists or more women?' *International Political Science Review*, **21**(4), pp. 381–405.

United Nations (1996) *The UN and the Advancement of Women 1945–1996*, rev. edn, Geneva: United Nations.

UNIFEM (2000) *Progress of the World's Women*, Biennial report, New York: UNIFEM.

Waylen, Georgina (1996) *Gender in Third World Politics*, Milton Keynes: Open University Press.

Wing, Adrien Katherine (ed.) (2000) *Global Critical Race Feminism: An International Reader (Critical America)*, New York: New York University Press.

Yates, Dianne (1998) 'Women in society', *The Parliamentarian*, **79**(3), pp. S24–S26.

Yuval-Davis, Nira and Anthias, Floya (eds) (1989) *Woman–Nation–State*, London: Macmillan.

Websites

Commonwealth Parliamentary Association
http://www.cpahq.org

Council of Europe
http://www.coe.int

European Database on Women and Decision Making
http://www.db-decision.de

Idea
http://www.idea.int/women/parl

Inter-Parliamentary Union
http://www.ipu.org

United Nations Development Fund for Women UNIFEM
http://www.unifem.undp.org

WSS Links Women and Gender Studies Websites
(This website links to hundreds of useful sources on women)
http://libraries.mit.edu/humanities/WomensStudies